Restoring
Hope

Restor

Conversations on the Future of Black America

A Project of the Obsidian Society

ing
Hope

Edited by
Kelvin Shawn Sealey

Cornel West

BEACON PRESS
25 Beacon Street
Boston, Massachusetts 02108-2892
http://www.beacon.org

BEACON PRESS BOOKS
are published under the auspices of
the Unitarian Universalist Association of Congregations.

"Catch the Fire" from *Wounded in the House of a Friend* by Sonia Sanchez, published
by Beacon Press. Copyright 1995 by Sonia Sanchez. Reprinted by permission of the
author.

02 01 00 99 98 97   8 7 6 5 4 3 2 1

Text design by Anne Chalmers
Composition by Wilsted & Taylor Publishing Services

Library of Congress Cataloging-in-Publication Data
West, Cornel.
    Restoring hope : conversations on the future of Black America /
Cornel West ; edited by Kelvin Shawn Sealey.
        p.   cm.
    "A project of the Obsidian Society."
    ISBN 0-8070-0942-3 (cloth)
    1. Afro-Americans—Social conditions.   2. Afro-Americans—Conduct
of life.   3. United States—Social conditions—1945–   4. Afro-
Americans—Interviews.   5. Celebrities—United States—Interviews.
    I. Sealey, Kelvin Shawn.   II. Title.
E185.86.W4385   1997
305.896'073—DC21   97-21797

To my beloved brother

REV. DR. JAMES MELVIN WASHINGTON

(1948–97)

An exemplary prisoner of hope in these desperate times

—CW

To

DOROTHY ELAINE BATSON-SEALEY

(1932–93)

—KSS

Contents

Foreword

RESTORING HOPE is a compelling collection of interviews—conversations or dialogues, really—with several of the
most fascinating figures in our country working in politics, religion, and the arts. The art of the interview, it seems to me, para-
doxically depends at once upon the presence of the interviewer
and his or her absence, silence, or invisibility. The role of an interviewer is somewhat that of a catalyst in a chemical equation:
elemental and essential, yet destined to disappear.

Cornel West's role, however, is not that of a traditional interviewer—unless we think of Socrates as the first great interlocu-
tor—for West's "interviews" with the subjects represented in
this marvelous volume are more akin to dialogues. Socratic in
their breadth and range, and in the truly dialectical manner in
which they unfold: two voices, two minds, a *pas de deux*, dancing
through a fertile field of ideas.

Cornel West's work has the greatest depth and versatility, a
rare combination, indeed, in any field. He preserves a truly or-
ganic link to the African American community without suc-
cumbing to vulgar nationalism or demagoguery, and without ig-
noring complexity. More than anyone else I can think of, he has
restored the full presence of the spoken human voice to the dis-

course of contemporary philosophy, the rhythmic structure of the performed word, the *philosophically* performed word.

West begins his conversation with Harry Belafonte, as he does with all his interviews in this series, with a question related to the concept of hope. The theme of hope is the leitmotif of the book. Throughout West attempts to outline the various notions of what hope means in America at the end of this century and, more specifically, what it means to African Americans and to the survival of African American culture.

The dialogues collected in *Restoring Hope*, taken together, represent a genuine contribution to the "conversation about race" upon which President Clinton, following a suggestion made by Lani Guinier, has urged us to embark. The diversity of opinions expressed here and the range of ideas touched upon reveal how very complex and subtle that conversation, at its best, can be. The richness of nuance in these discourses is a testament to Cornel West's own extraordinary capacity to give a voice to the *Zeitgeist*, and to enable us to find our own.

HENRY LOUIS GATES, JR.

Preface

He who has never despaired has no need to have lived.   —Goethe

A SPECTER of despair haunts late twentieth-century America. The quality of our lives and the integrity of our souls are in jeopardy. Wealth inequality and class polarization are escalating—with ugly consequences for the most vulnerable among us. The lethal power of global corporate elites and national managerial bosses is at an all-time high. Spiritual malnutrition and existential emptiness are rampant. The precious systems of caring and nurturing are eroding. Market moralities and mentalities—fueled by economic imperatives to make a profit at nearly any cost—yield unprecedented levels of loneliness, isolation, and sadness. And our public life lies in shambles, shot through with icy cynicism and paralyzing pessimism. To put it bluntly, beneath the record-breaking stock markets on Wall Street and bipartisan budget-balancing deals in the White House lurk ominous clouds of despair across this nation.

This bleak portrait is accentuated in black America. The fragile black middle class—always a *lumpenbourgeoisie* in America—fights a white backlash. The devastated black working class fears further underemployment or unemployment. And the besieged black poor struggle to survive. Nearly thirty years after the cowardly murder of Martin Luther King, Jr., black America sits on the brink of collective disaster.

Yet most of our fellow citizens deny this black despair, downplay this black rage, and blind themselves to the omens in our midst. So now, as in the past, we prisoners of hope in desperate times must try to speak our fallible truths, expose the vicious lies, and bear our imperfect witness.

This book is a kind of wake-up call to each of us. The country is in deep trouble. We need a moral prophetic minority of all colors who muster the courage to question the powers that be, the courage to be impatient with evil and patient with people, and the courage to fight for social justice. Such courage rests on a deep democratic vision of a better world that lures us and a blood-drenched hope that sustains us.

This hope is not the same as optimism. Optimism adopts the role of the spectator who surveys the evidence in order to infer that things are going to get better. Yet we know that the evidence does not look good. The dominant tendencies of our day are unregulated global capitalism, racial balkanization, social breakdown, and individual depression. Hope enacts the stance of the participant who actively struggles against the evidence in order to change the deadly tides of wealth inequality, group xenophobia, and personal despair. Only a new wave of vision, courage, and hope can keep us sane—and preserve the decency and dignity requisite to revitalize our organizational energy for the work to be done. To live is to wrestle with despair yet never to allow despair to have the last word.

CORNEL WEST

Introduction

THE STORY behind the construction of this book is itself, like the book's theme, a lesson in the possibility of hope. And so it should be, for the act of hoping has sustained many an American of African descent throughout history, producing words, pictures, memories, and opportunities, much like this volume, from which many have profited. While born of an individual idea, *Restoring Hope* was a great collective, altruistic effort, one that intends to speak to the hearts and minds of Americans anxious for new signs of human concern for the social and spiritual well-being of Americans of all races. We begin, then, with the idea out of which *Restoring Hope* grew and of which you, the reader, have now become an intimate part.

Several years ago, the actor Paul Newman made the decision to invest a part of his wealth, time, and considerable public appeal in the creation of a food products manufacturing company whose profits would be dedicated to charities working on behalf of children. I was approximately twenty when the first announcements were made and was touched by the generosity Mr. Newman showed the world. Having accomplished much in his life, he saw the need to give back some of what he had earned to those less fortunate than he had been. This is, I believe, a genuine

American sentiment, one that I felt the need to emulate even as I heard it articulated for the first time. Newman's Own, which has sold millions of dollars of popcorn, salad dressing, spaghetti sauce, and other products over the last fourteen years, would become the model for a venture I was fated to begin.

The model is simple: in the entrepreneurially rich country that we inhabit, one is just as capable of beginning a business for personal as for charitable ends. To the extent that an idea is viable, that the entrepreneur understands the rigors of starting and running a business—the critical ingredient being determination and perseverance—that entrepreneur stands a good chance of seeing his or her idea come to fruition, producing profits that can then be used for any purpose. While Paul Newman chose children as his beneficiaries, I took a hard look at the position of African Americans and considered beginning a philanthropic organization that would serve their interests.

The African American condition, if one uses the date of the original importation of Africans to North America, is 378 years old as of 1997. It has been a difficult, tumultuous, extraordinary, painful, harrowing, beautiful, and hopeful condition, to say the least. In this, it follows the history of most people in the world, being simultaneously complex, frightful, and moving. But, unlike many other people, African Americans have been subject to the debasing and largely unrelieved burdens of racism and racial discrimination against which we have fought an unending battle. We have, together with those concerned with the American condition generally, managed to move toward a position of greater equity and possibility, even as our enemies—the enemies of fairness and justice—would have us maintained in a state of impoverishment and despair.

This was not, nor shall it ever be, our permanent condition as Americans. Like the millions who came to these shores purposefully, African Americans have long sought everything good that there was and is to seek within the folds of this nation. With our hopes partially fulfilled, the idea of further progress compelled me to seek solutions to the modern state of the African American condition, a condition that was viable and sustainable in some quarters but that could be greatly improved by the concentrated effort of people and institutions dedicated to its betterment. By too many measures, the black condition is vastly in need of improvement.

Thus was born the idea for the Obsidian Society, a not-for-profit foundation that intends to work toward the improvement of the African American condition. This, I agree, is a tall order, but not so tall that it cannot be accomplished successfully. What I intend to do is give support, both in-kind and financial, to individuals and organizations committed to improving and sustaining the material conditions of Americans of African descent in the critical areas of the arts, education, and the social services. Philanthropy, the act of giving capital resources to those in need, is an activity engaged in by Americans far more often than by any other people in the world. As an American, and as an African American, it is my responsibility both to support the act of philanthropy and to further its growth within black communities. Here I am only acting much as our people have acted since our seventeenth-century beginnings.

The Obsidian Society intends to draw its resources partly from independent for-profit companies, a portion of whose profits will be dedicated to the support of the society's ends. Likewise, I have begun creating a series of companies whose sole end is creating money for the society, in a process called entrepreneurial philanthropy, a phrase coined by Dr. Kathleen McCarthy at the Center for the Study of Philanthropy at the City University of New York Graduate Center. To engage in for-profit business for not-for-profit ends is, I believe, an idea ripe with possibility for many segments of society, particularly as government aid has been summarily reduced for or withdrawn from many organizations traditionally supported by the state. The Obsidian Society intends to present a model of how for-profit and not-for-profit activity may be harmoniously merged.

This brings us, in circuitous fashion, to the restoration of hope in African American communities (plural here because there is not now and never has been one, single, monolithic African American community), the subject of this book. When I approached Dr. Cornel West in the fall of 1993 with my idea for the Obsidian Society, he generously agreed to help me build it from the ground up. His acceptance of my idea changed my life and produced the work you hold in your hands. It was my suggestion to Dr. West that he and I produce a book in which we explored, with several notable Americans, the idea of hope in black America and how it could be restored and sustained. Produced as a series of public dialogues, *Restoring Hope* took shape as the first for-profit venture under the banner of the Obsidian Society.

Obsidian, Inc., the holding company with which the Obsidian Society works, intends to take on projects in the literary, entertainment, new media, and finance industries. To the extent that feature, cable, and made-for-television movies, television shows, record albums, computer games, and mutual funds have ready markets in America or around the world, the flow of profits into the Obsidian Society will continue. Although in its infancy, Obsidian hopes to exploit the exciting growth that we are seeing in these vastly internationalized industries. The broad sweep of American capitalism presents a ready opportunity for those willing to devote a portion—or all—of their profits to not-for-profit ends, particularly if it helps aid the further development of the nation. Financing scholarships, dance and other arts, and social programs for children and families will indeed strengthen American society and contribute to the dynamism that has brought us across more than two hundred years of nationhood.

In the name of Obsidian, then, the distinguished list of Americans who answered our call stands as a testament to the strength of altruism in this country and among African Americans. I am grateful to all of them for the generosity of their spirits and the gift of their time. All our dialogue partners responded with an enthusiasm that was heartwarming and appreciated. They have proved to me that the idea of giving is sound and that, when called on, Americans will respond to the opportunity to give as will no other nationality in the world.

How, then, can we tie the restoraton of hope in African America to philanthropy and altruism? As dedicated as we Americans are to the pursuit of financial gain, and recognizing our allegiance to the mighty system of capitalist economics that brings us our wealth and our poverty, it behooves us to tie the idea of hope to the idea of capital. If we are to hope for anything, whether black, white, Asian, Native, or Latin, that hope must in some way be tied to aspirations for material improvement. While it is certainly true that political, social, and racial equality has eluded many who have fought for it over the course of centuries, it is even more true that the realm of economics may help bring many of the other problems in line. Our attempts to legislate away the stain of racism and discrimination having failed, pattern and practice suggest that Americans will respond to capital as they will respond to nothing else. Those who have lost hope or who remain hopeless in the face of new economic and social hostilities must come to believe that new economic mechanisms for social equality are actively being developed. I do not say this lightly; it is in the interest of all Americans that the problems that we face be debated far more extensively and regularly than is now the case. Solutions must be backed by solid, viable, sustainable means by which we can put into practice mechanisms for improving lives, lives that might otherwise be lost to the treachery of misguidance. And here I am thinking of the many American children who live in poverty, who go hungry every day, who live without heat and hot water in the winter. We must attend to these matters.

Connecting the idea of hope to the lesson of giving is critical. Enlarging the picture to include ideas for how capitalism, altruism, and hope can form a meaningful composite rounds out the picture I have been trying to draw and lays out the prime impulse of the Obsidian Society. In this great nation of ours, more must be done consciously to invite the entrepreneurial, altruistic, and philanthropic public to connect to the section of the population that has lost or is losing hope. The Obsidian Society, a newborn in the world of philanthropy, hopes to represent one form of opportunity. We believe that we can help sustain emerging successes in the arts, education, and social services. From that sustenance may spring further ideas for change. Further, we believe that this can be done with a dedicated multiracial, gendered, youthful and mature, international organization. Not merely as a matter of conscience, race, or charity, the Obsidian Society and its staff, volunteers, and corporate and individual partners understand the integrity of the larger web of life of which we are all an intimate part. That web, for its long-term well-being, its growth, its hope, and its life, must be regularly infused with the stuff of dreams. Life is too important for us to do anything less. And I am, at thirty-five years old, not about to see lost the work of fifty million souls over five centuries evaporate in the whirlwind of twentieth-century consumer and capitalist greed. This generation of Americans, and particularly Americans of African descent, must take up the mantle of those who came before and move ahead. And once we reach the next level, I suspect, we shall discover how to move even higher.

It is a good time to be an American. Unrivaled prosperity dominates the land, and many of the ghosts of our past are being confronted with new passion. Yet poverty and despair, about which my colleague Cornel West regularly reminds us, are also growing with biblical certainty. The challenge remains to harness the power of prosperity and turn it to overcoming poverty and despair. While over time a few societies have found creative ways of grappling with the problem, none have solved it, and fewer still show signs of coming close to a solution any time soon. Our work, then, is cut out for us, and I am here to say that we can, as an entrepreneurial nation, find a way to pursue our dreams while still doing some material good for those prosperity has left behind. To continue to ignore the less fortunate among us will place the nation in peril. The Obsidian Society, and those who would support its efforts, does not wish for our prosperity to end or for the hungry to remain without food. We do not see it as an either-or situation. And we are working toward solutions that would both maintain our prosperity and feed our hungry. No more could be asked of us; no more would be necessary.

KELVIN SHAWN SEALEY

Harry Belafonte

3 June 1996, Schomburg Center, New York

CORNEL WEST: Let's begin with what it means to be an artist, especially in the context of an oppressed people?

HARRY BELAFONTE: I think that there was a great coincidence in my life because of the time in which I grew up. America was fermenting. The Great Depression was on. Everybody was ground under. And the whole thrust to change the human condition, to deal with big business, to deal with monopoly capital, introduced into the American cultural psyche a whole language and a whole debate that was very, very heavily socialist in its rhythm and in its character. And when you read all the great writers of the period, all of them were great social writers—Steinbeck and Hemingway, for example.

And then I began to read Dr. Du Bois and what he wrote about Africa. And the dialogue that was going on, and all the art of the period out of the WPA, was really about the condition and the life of workers. So that in the labor movement, when you think of great painters like Charlie White or great dancers like Katherine Dunham, all of those people came out of the WPA, that late thirties, early forties period. America was rich and vibrant and full of protest. And it was the thing to do. As a matter of fact, all the later movies in Hollywood in that period, and especially during the war, propagandized very heavily: We should hate fascism. We should embrace the Russians. They are our allies. We should be there together in the struggle, to unify. All those things were part of the pollination of the period. It was just rampant. And I got caught up in that. I heard that, I tasted it. And to me there was just no question that we were in the moment of our greatest liberation and our greatest opportunity.

All that was part of the environment. So for me art and politics were synonymous. As a matter of fact, if art was not political, to me it wasn't even art. It was Paul Robeson who once said to me, "The purpose of art is not just to show life as it is but to show life as it should be." That became my motto. And very early on when I turned to singing and he came to hear concerts of mine, he said, "Harry, get them to sing your song. And then they'll have to come to know who you are."

When I sing "The Banana Boat Song," most people see it as some whimsical, fanciful little tale that brings charm and delight to the listener. But to me, it's about a human condition that was very real to me as a child in Jamaica and very painful and extremely oppressive. Most of my family were plantation workers, working on land owned by British nobility who were not living on the island. They chopped sugarcane, and chopped bananas, and loaded ships, and did all these things under tremendous difficulty and pain and anguish. But they did it also with strength and hope. And in that context they would sing. They would sing because, as was known by almost every member of the diaspora, song was sometimes our only relief from the burden of life. And we could communicate and tell tales and aspire to greater things.

I always thought that if people came to embrace my art and began to sing my song, they would want to know who I am. And if I could get them to the next level of that curiosity, I would politicize them to death. When my mother brought me back to America from Jamaica as a child, I found many of the people in my community in Harlem wrapped around the radio. We couldn't wait to go to the theaters in and around the 125th Street area: the Harlem Opera House, the RKO Regency. We used to go up to the West End Theater. And we would see whatever it was that Hollywood had put out, and we saw that as the only art that was available. At the time the only art I knew of was art that propagandized and told stories about the human condition—the art of the movies, the art of radio and what radio disseminated as the truth and the values of the day.

My earliest knowledge of people of Africa, for instance, was really through the Tarzan movies. The very first Tarzan movie I saw was in 1935, *Tarzan and the Apes*. I went to see this film about this place called Africa, with these people of color who were steeped in ignorance, steeped in folly, steeped in the absence of any articulation whatsoever, and were not redeemable except when the great white hero came swinging through the trees and landed in the midst of them to give them direction and to describe life as they should aspire to it.

For a long time I thought of Africa as a place I really did not want to be. Those were people that I would just as soon not know. And it was strange that so many people in my own community looked like them or something like them. And how lucky they were to have had white leadership to help them.

That was a bit of art—albeit bad art. But it was nevertheless a force that imparted information and helped me begin to think

about art. Other Hollywood films I saw depicted people of color
in some deeply demeaning way. Especially people who were portrayed on the screen as domestics. I saw no nobility in them. I saw
no courage, I saw no strength. I saw only people who were in the
service of and in debt to their white masters. Of course my
mother, who was a domestic worker, who was extremely feisty,
who was extremely aggressive in her social and political views,
gave me other thoughts and other concepts.

So early on, I saw great differences between truth and fiction—or between truth and other truths. And as I watched Hollywood and I watched popular art vehicles of the period—magazines that told stories every now and then about us; certainly the
radio, which gave us great heroes like Amos and Andy and Jack
Benny's servant, Rochester—there was hardly a thing that I
heard about or saw in black people and people of color as they
were portrayed that didn't leave me with an enormous sense of
frustration and dissatisfaction. Although at that point to be an
artist myself was the furthest thing from my mind.

When I was born, in 1927, it was the very year that Marcus
Garvey was being deported from the United States. Marcus Garvey being a Jamaican gave us some sense of glory, gave us some
sense of being people of thought and reason. So I caught up on
all the Garvey stories and information and memories, which
were still quite active in the Harlem community with people
talking about what we could and should be doing as a people—
especially within the West Indian community, which had a very
special place here in Harlem.

But then in 1939 I saw a newsreel—it was in either the Harlem
Opera House or the West End—on Emperor Haile Selassie and

the fascist troops from Italy who were getting ready to invade Ethiopia. Here were pictures of the mechanized divisions of the Italian army rolling through the Ethiopian countryside, victoriously, crushing peasant soldiers, barefoot soldiers, men who stood up for their homeland, fighting these tanks with spears. I realized that the rest of the world saw great nobility in resistance to this oppressive thing that was going on. I saw Haile Selassie's appeal to the League of Nations. And I saw in this man a contradiction to everything I had understood about Africa. I saw in him dignity, enormous majesty, and pride. Here was an African man speaking most profoundly and articulately to an august body of world leaders, begging them for their intervention on behalf of his nation. Predicting that if they did not intervene, they would soon be paying the price that his nation was paying for the onslaught of fascism.

So alien to me was the Haile Selassie world, the Haile Selassie image, that once I saw it, I became very curious. And I asked a lot of questions of a lot of people. They gave me a lot of answers, many of them contradictory, very varied. All those questions led to other questions. I always had a need to know. I always wanted to know, even in my youngest years.

Now that pursuit became somewhat conflicted because I suffered from a learning disorder, a thing called dyslexia. Most people didn't understand that disorder back then. All they saw was this young boy who appeared to have an agreeable amount of intelligence, who was not applying himself, who would not study, who would not read, who would not attend to the gift of instruction, and who seemed to have no need to want to deal with the institutions of learning. So in public school I was quite distracted, I was quite uncomfortable. My mother was constantly coming to school. And I never went to high school, as a matter of fact. The journey was just so extremely painful.

So that time in my life was the period during which I discovered not only Tarzan and Africa, but Haile Selassie and Africa, and Marcus Garvey, and asked all these questions. And then of course the experiences that we had when we constantly read, especially in the black newspapers, *The Age* and the *Amsterdam News*, about the lynchings and the oppressive violence going on in other parts of America, where our kinfolk and others were being systematically murdered and destroyed and imprisoned. Nobody seemed to be there to give us relief from all of this. So I understood early on that since there was no one to help us, and since the condition was so painful, it was most likely up to us to go ahead and help ourselves. From that moment on, I began to look for expressions of that kind of thought, for men and women who embodied that spirit of rebellion, that spirit of protest, that thing that came up against the system that was so oppressive. And in that pursuit I had a series of encounters that led me to the world of art and the power of art.

CW: You're fifteen years old at this point, though, right? Now, where did that come from, that depth of curiosity as well as, I would think, this tremendous sense of, belief in, self? Was that rooted in family? Was that rooted in community? Where did it come from, that little Harry could actually take on the world like that?

HB: My mother was responsible for most of that. When she got through instructing me and telling me what I would be responsible for in the world, I understood at the age of nine that I was, in fact, singularly responsible for black liberation. [*Laughter. Ap-*

plause.] My mother's name was Millie, and she was really quite a remarkable woman. She was never formally educated. She came here at the age of fifteen as an immigrant from Jamaica because many in Jamaica had heard that it was possible to do well in that big place up in the north and that the West Indian community here was beginning to carve out some kind of meaningful life for itself, especially members of our family. And when my mother came here, seeking to become part of that mission and that purpose, she found like everyone else that the story was more fiction than fact, that life here was extremely difficult and terribly oppressive.

My mother used to go down to Park Avenue where the Grand Central Station El came out of the tunnel and went above ground. Now, she would go there any time of the year—summer, spring, winter, fall—and stand in line with hundreds and hundreds of other black women, dressed as neatly as they could, while white woman from downtown, or sometimes their maids, would pass down the line and pick the worker of the day, or the worker of the weekend. And that was how my mother was able to gain employment as a domestic worker.

And when my mother came back from her domestic work, and when she came back from other encounters with the white world, she would speak to her children. And she would tell us stories of her experiences. And she would show us the newspapers, and she would point to the pictures and tell us who the good guys were and who the bad guys were. And tell us what the papers were saying. She would slowly and painfully read through and give us some sense of the world in which we lived.

So she was constantly talking, and constantly analyzing, and constantly instructing. And we went to the movies. And I came back and asked her all about Haile Selassie. What she didn't know she would go out and learn so she could give me some answers. She used to go right here to the YWCA on 135th Street, and she took sewing classes, and she took reading classes. And she always looked for literature that would help tell her more about the world and its condition.

She had the burden of trying to bring up her children, and shunting us back and forth to the West Indies, and doing it very nervously. Her last trip was 1939, the year the war broke out between England and Germany. She brought us back, my brother and I, because she thought that Germany might very well win the war. And if the Germans won the war, then that meant that all British colonies would be under German rule, and she didn't want her children there.

The American government and American society were in a new moment. The Great Depression had forced this country to put resources into the development of culture and people, to open up the work process to let people in. The Congress of Industrial Organization was organizing in the South. The stories were running rampant throughout our community about all these things that were exploding everywhere. So for me it was a time of great excitement. And I went to a movie because that was my favorite thing to do, to go to the movies. It was instructive, it was a chance to escape. And I saw a film called *Sahara*, put out by Columbia Pictures. The director was a man by the name of Courter, an Englishman. It starred Humphrey Bogart. And this picture was about an American tank unit, fighting in North Africa against the fascists, that had lost its way and gotten separated from its unit in the midst of this desert. And it had picked up some stragglers from other Allied forces, one of them being an African who was with the British forces as a Sudanese soldier. He was played by Rex Ingram. And when I went to see this movie— it was just a war flick—this black man reminded me very much of Haile Selassie. He had great dignity, he was very articulate, and he was not at all, in anything that he did in this film, subservient. I watched him very closely because I'd never seen him or anyone like him on the screen before.

In the picture, the Allies had captured a Nazi pilot. And as the plot went on, the troops were looking for water, and they discovered that there was a huge German regiment moving up on the same oasis. The Allies had one tank. The well was not filled with as much water as everybody thought, but they had to make the Germans, who were very thirsty, according to the plot, think that they had all the water. And the only way the Germans could get it would be to surrender. That's Hollywood. [*Laughter.*] But the German pilot escaped and was on his way to German lines to tell the Germans that the whole thing was false—that they could storm the tank and capture it. And here came the great moment: it was the Sudanese soldier who broke ranks with the Allied troops, chased after this German soldier, and tackled him. Even as bullets were riddling the soldier's body, he put his black hand into the blond hair of this white Nazi soldier, buried his face in the sand, and snuffed out his life. And just before dying, the soldier put his thumb up to send a signal back to the Allied forces that his mission had been completed.

That had a profound effect on me. I had never, ever, ever seen a black man kill a white man. Certainly never as an act of great heroism and nobility for which he was embraced by white folk.

CW: Did they clap for him?

HB: The white folk at the Roxy Theater where I saw it were just applauding to death. And I looked around, sitting in the balcony. It was then that I realized what the power of acting could do. Here was a story, very richly designed in the cinema style. And here was this man, Rex Ingram, playing this part of enormous strength and dignity. It was no small moment for me because it convinced me that I should do everything that Rex Ingram did [*laughter*], both over there and when I came back home. That's when I volunteered.

When I entered into the Second World War, it was the first time I discovered diversity among black people. Because the only people that I really knew were members of the Harlem community, and they had a very special style, a very special way. There were the Harlem folk and the West Indian folk who were in Harlem. And those were the two people that I knew, the two groups that I knew, the two cultures that I knew. When I went into the navy, however, I found black people from Mississippi; from Memphis, Tennessee; from Chicago. Everybody spoke different, everybody looked different. Everybody had different things to say, different tastes, different foods. I had never understood before that there was this enormous diversity among us as a people in this one country. I thought all of us would be just like we were—

CW: Just like in Harlem.

HB: Yes. And it was in this context that I got my first exposure to intellectuals, black intellectuals. It was in this context that I was first given to read a book written by Dr. W. E. B. Du Bois. I hung around with this group in my outfit who were intellectuals, college graduates.

CW: Which book was this?

HB: It was *Color and Democracy.* The soldiers who gave me the book to read really threw it to me like giving a dog a bone because I was the youngest member of the group. I was always asking questions, and I got the feeling that they were very annoyed with me. So they gave me the book really to silence me. [*Laughter.*] Like, man, go read. I had this reading disorder, and I struggled through the book. As I read the book, I noticed that at the end of certain sentences and passages there was a number. And I was too intimidated to ask them what the number meant. I didn't want any more insults. So I struggled on. And I realized that every time I saw a number on the page, if I looked at the foot of the page, there was a corollary, and it often referred to the work that he was referring to, you know, some quote. And I decided that since this man Du Bois, whom they had spoken about so often, was so learned—and my mother had once or twice mentioned him because he was the founder of the NAACP, which she loved and thought was doing good work—I just said, Well, when I get my first leave, I'll go into Chicago, go to the library, and I'll just get the books that I saw at the foot of the page. Since this was material that was instructing Du Bois, and he was this omnipotent brain, certainly I could do no worse than to read these books and better my own knowledge.

So I made this list. But I noticed one thing as I went along: how often I saw the name "Ibid." [*Laughter.*] Du Bois had a lot of

Ibids. I decided that that was certainly one of the books, one of
the writers, I should get. [*Laughter.*] So when I went to Chicago,
I gave my dog tag number and registered in the library. A little
white lady, I'll never forget, a very old white lady, was the librarian. I gave her my list, and she said, "Well, young man, this is far
too many books for you to take, even with your military privileges. So you'll just have to narrow that list down before I can deal
with it." So I said, "Well, I'll make your life easy. Just give me the
few books you have by Ibid." [*Laughter.*] She pointed out that
there was no such writer. And I insisted that there was because
Du Bois said that there was. She went to the index, and came
back, and said, "There's no such author." And I said there was.
And she got very annoyed and said she didn't want to discuss it
any longer, and I denounced her as a racist. When I got back to
the barracks, I told the men what happened to me. [*Laughter.*]
They fell out, they laughed. And they told me of my folly. I went
back to that library looking for that little white lady so I could
apologize to her.

It was a rhythm of all these things. In the navy I met artists, I
met musicians, I met poets, I met writers. And I saw Rex Ingram,
and began to learn about what the theater was, and then came
back to Harlem and to the library in the Schomburg Center in
pursuit of knowledge. I then discovered the American Negro
Theater down in the basement. And as a matter of fact, I was
given two tickets as a gratuity. I was a janitor's assistant. And when
I repaired something in an apartment, the woman who was the
tenant of the apartment gave me these two tickets, and I came to
the theater. She was in the play. A lot of people might remember
her. Her name was Clarisse Taylor.

CW: That's not *Home Is the Hunter?*

HB: *Home Is the Hunter* is the name of the play. And I saw the play. And when I sat in the theater next door, it was absolutely as magical a moment for me as seeing Haile Selassie on the screen. And I realized when I saw that theater, and I saw the black actors, and I saw what they were saying, that the theater was the place that I wanted to be. I wanted to belong to that. It said something. It moved people. It could inspire. It sang magically. So I joined up with the group as a stagehand and then got involved. And I used the GI Bill and went to school and then went on with my life acting.

I understood that power when I met Paul Robeson. Robeson came to the American Negro Theater one night. We knew of him. We knew of all the things that he did and had said. But when he came to the play that we were in—we were doing a play by Sean O'Casey, an Irish playwright, and the play was called *Juno and the Paycock*—Robeson talked to us at the end of the evening. And his nobility and his language and his encouragement and his praise put me forever in his debt because it inspired me fully to know that this would be my life. And to be like him, and to use my life as he had used his, and to put into it the commitment of the liberation of his people and all people. And to relate to all the artists to whom he related became my own mission. So I stayed very close to Paul from those days until his death. I then got to meet Dr. Du Bois and spend time with him in Brooklyn. I then met all of the great writers in and around New York—Langston Hughes, James Baldwin, and all the others.

CW: Now, you were close to many musicians, too, like Duke Ellington and the great Louis Armstrong. How did you negotiate these relationships so that you could revel in the genius of the jazz musicians when it looked as if they were less political than you were? Were they less political?

HB: I've always believed that the culture of a people is the soul of a people. It expresses their highest hopes and aspirations. And in that hope, and in that aspiration, there is a political statement. So that if someone is overtly political or artistically great and speaks to the human condition in a way that illuminates and inspires, I see that also as a political consequence or a political act. When I went down to the Royal Roost, I saw Charlie Parker and Max Roche and all the young men who played, and I saw Billie Holliday. And Billie Holliday, after all, had been the great voice of our time as an artist, and she was the one who sang "Strange Fruit" and had a great impact on us in that period. She used her art to speak to the suffering of black people in a very direct way.

So when I went into this environment, I'd already accepted the fact that our art was the substance of our soul and our survival because it was our art that permitted us to survive. I understood through Du Bois and the books that I read that had it not been for our art and our culture, when all else was ripped from us, we would never have been able to survive as a people. Through our songs, even—because all of our songs are filled with metaphor and filled with subtext, and we're always codifying. And I always saw jazz as not only an expression of ourselves but also an expression of our protest. And when I went to see Charlie Parker, I didn't realize in the beginning that someday I'd wind up singing for him and with him. But we talked in the late hours of the morning because I stayed at the club until the last minute. I sometimes did my homework in the club when I had an analysis to do for the theater. Because out there they closed at eleven o'clock at night when the plays were all going to be wrapped as sets. So I could then go immediately to the Royal Roost and hang out. And I did this for a couple of years.

As I got to know Charlie Parker and to talk, it was just around 1948 when the Young Progressives of America, which I belonged to, were mobilizing people. And Paul Robeson was on his march. And I went out and conned all these guys into coming in and playing for our rallies. Charlie Parker went with me many a night to Brooklyn and to Harlem and to places just to play before Du Bois spoke and before Robeson spoke. And once he did it, he began to say, "Hey, Harry man, you get any more of them gigs, call me."

CW: And that was on political grounds?

HB: Oh, very much so. Very much so.

CW: No cash flow.

HB: No, no. No cash flow at all.

CW: That's interesting. Well, let's look at the contemporary situation. You say that culture is the substance of a people, it helps them survive, it soothes their bruises and allows them to transfigure and transmute their sadness into imaginative form. I think about you organizing in 1948 a rally to bring in the great artists, in 1963 the great march with Brother Martin Luther King, Jr., bringing in Mahalia Jackson, Sammy Davis Jr., Lena Horne, and so many other great artists as well. Now when we look in the nineties at black culture, black music, black literature, black plays, and so forth, when you look at the present situation and the talented young brothers and sisters—Chuck D, KRS-ONE, Anita Baker, and others—what do you see now? Do you see the same depth? Is it different? Or does the survival of black folk as reflected in our culture seem to be more tenuous now than it was when we had the Charlie Parkers and the Coltranes and the Sarah Vaughns and others?

HB: I think that we are in the greatest jeopardy we have ever been in. I really believe that. I am really quite troubled at what I see. Although we have been in dark periods before—certainly no period in the existence of black people could possibly have been more dark and more wretched and more hopeless than the slave period down in the holds of ships, stacked there, brought to this strange place and so brutally treated for so many centuries; certainly there must have been a sense that there was just no hope, that God had really forsaken us, if in fact there was a God. Because how could you live through all that? And I tend to think that there may be divine intervention at the end of this period through which we will be going.

What makes the crisis for me so great is that I see a whole people being wasted and being denied and being suffocated. I think black culture as it sits in America, and as it sits in other places in the diaspora, is under the greatest onslaught of negativity that has ever existed because of what monopoly capital is doing to control all the forces that buy and sell art, and determine the tastes of the public, and instruct and condition people in a way even Orwell didn't quite imagine. I think it is far more drastic than anything Orwell thought of in his book. And it is this that troubles me. Because technology in the hands of the oppressor is the new legacy to domination in the future. And that fact alone, I think, has done much to neuter blacks as a people, and in fact it affects everybody—black, white. It isn't just black folk who are suffering from this. I think all Americans suffer from it. Anyone who has played a game with that cultural imperialism is doomed by it.

When I was a boy growing up, I could go anywhere in black America and find blues, find jazz, find hoke, find all kinds of things that I would take and extract, get experiences from, and be stimulated by. I don't know where to go today. There are no clubs. There are a handful of discos. We can go downtown to a few places that keep it alive. But by and large, we have been integrated out of culture. And those who are successful in that world have no sensitivity or commitment to this loss and this pain because they have become the new class elite. And in their class interests, all they want to do is to continue to perpetually make movies that will be successful at the box office on Hollywood's terms, on the bank's terms, and all the while they watch their culture die, and young people have nothing to look to. When I look at television, I see what black families are required to do in sitcoms especially—what they say, how they behave, how that must absolutely, completely satisfy the appetite of white America, and if it doesn't, it will not get on the air. And those who are being paid to do it, who want to live and get on the air and have money, play the game. So it's a Catch-22. Everybody's caught in a circle of self-destruction. And it isn't just we as black people who are being destroyed. It's a nation that's being destroyed because we are becoming uniculture. We all have the same tastes, we all speak for the same thing. We think we're all informed because we all saw the same TV show. So when we get up in the morning, we can tell each other what we saw. As opposed to what we really know.

CW: That's right, that's right.

HB: We don't go to books anymore. Once in a while I can catch some-
       thing on the Discovery channel that might give me a little illumi-
       nation. I must say public broadcasting gives us a blessing here and
       there. They let you and Henry Louis Gates talk on Charlie Rose.
       But in terms of art, we have no place on television—no weekly
       program that does nothing but deal with jazz, deal with blues,
       deal with gospel, just deal with culture. All this could be dissemi-
       nated and make a change, I think; it puts the handwriting on
       the wall.
            When Dr. King stepped onto the new level of the struggle,
       which we identify as the civil rights movement, there were fewer
       than three hundred black elected officials in this country, and
       most of them were on the lowest rung of the political ladder—
       the lowest. We had a handful of men, three or four, who sat in our
       Congress: Adam Clayton Powell and the others. But beyond that
       there was nothing. Today there are over eight thousand black
       people who have successfully engaged the political process of
       electoral politics. If anybody had told me thirty years ago when
       this campaign was on that we'd wind up with governors, and sen-
       ators, and mayors, and people in state legislatures, and in the
       Congress, and in the Senate, and in other branches of govern-
       ment, sitting in the cabinet, in the military, and we would not be
       able to make a vast difference in how black people are experienc-
       ing life, I'd have said you're smoking dope. You know, you don't
       understand. History isn't going to do that to us. All we need is
       black people in the right places, and they will make a difference.
       And I believed in that so strongly; I really did. And I tell you, I've
       been from corporate America to corporate America. I've seen
       black people sitting up in the highest of places. I know some guys

who are a heartbeat away from becoming the chief executive officer of some of the biggest companies in this country, who don't give a damn about the black condition.

CW: That's quite an irony, isn't it? That after all this progress owing to blood, sweat, and tears, there seems to be less hope in black America than there was in the late fifties and early sixties, when you were coming along, in which this progressive tide was emerging. What do we say to young people? For example, let's take a young brother just like yourself, living right around the corner from here, seized by the life of the mind, excited by art the same way you were owing to your mother and others. What would be the journey, the pilgrimage, the trajectory, for such a young brother these days?

HB: Well, there are two things I'd have to say. The last time I spoke to Paul Robeson was at his home in Philadelphia. He was quite beat up by then, and broken, and quite ill.

I talked to him about sacrifice. And I said to him, "Paul, was it worth it? The price you paid with the House Un-American Activities Committee, what they did to you? The way all your colleagues in the black community, the black elite, and the black intellectuals, how they distanced themselves from you? How they never sought to support you and to praise you? All that you've been through? Was the journey, in the final analysis, worth it?" And he said, "Absolutely." "There may have been moments when things were painful," he said, "but even with the victories that we didn't achieve, the journey was worth it because I met so many magnificent men and women on the way who made it all worthwhile." He said, "However, there's one thing that I wish I had known then that I know now." And I said, "What is it?" He said,

"Harry, in the final analysis, every generation must be responsible for itself."

I think that, in a way, with all that we try to do and what we say we try to leave as a legacy, those of us who are trying to leave something, that young man that you've just described has got to find you, Cornel. Somewhere along the line, somebody's got to give him a dollar so he can get somewhere to hear you speak or to find out where I am when I'm doing my thing. You know, even today, when I read what was going on in Rwanda, I made it my business to go there three weeks after that war had escalated— because I didn't want the *New York Times*, and I didn't want Bill Clinton, and I didn't want George Bush or anybody else to tell me about what black folk were doing to black folk. I had to go see it for myself. And I think there's got to be more personal initiative among young people to want to find the greater truth. Because I know they're in pain. They've got to be in pain. There's too much destruction out there. There's too much confusion out there. And I think we've got to turn them around and let them come to the institutions. Right here in this library, this room right now should be jammed with young people. They're not here.

This room would be jammed with young people if we had a rap act going on, you know, or we had some other form of entertainment, because we've become an entertainment people. Entertain us, and we will listen. If you can't entertain us, we have no use for you. And we've just got to get out of that. The church, I think, has played a devastatingly poor role in leading the young of this country. Dr. King always talked about the failure of the clergy to have been in the vanguard of instruction. Because what are the churches doing? I know there are some individuals whom we can exempt from that. But by and large the millions and millions of black people in the diaspora who are Christians can easily say, I think, without fear of contradiction, that Christianity has played no serious role in their liberation, not today. The closest they came was Dr. King, and even Dr. King had to write the letter from a Birmingham jail criticizing the clergy for how they had denied him and denounced the movement. Where is all of it? I think that we just have to find it, and young people are going to have to get out there and do it.

But I think that the liberatory impulse among young people has seriously decreased because it has been replaced by something else that was never meant to be. When we talked about integration, we were talking about the ending of segregation and the right to opportunity. We wanted to integrate so that we could have the right to opportunity. What in fact happened in that quest and in the immediate successes of it was that we integrated and lost our cultural base. Every movie house in Harlem that I went to as a kid automatically closed. There wasn't a movie house in Harlem anywhere for almost twenty years. And every time kids wanted to go to the movies, they went downtown because now we were integrated. When we were integrating, we talked about getting into the life of mainstream America, which meant into the life of white America. We were already into the life of black mainstream America. So when you talk about mainstream America and all those titles to which everyone aspires, it means getting into white America and doing those things that white America will accept and approve of. And every step of the way we have been forced to deny more and more who we are and what we are, as a culture, as a people, as a history, as a race. As we integrate into it, we find more things that are valueless—valueless.

The last thing Dr. King ever said to me he said standing in my home just before he went down to Memphis. We had strategized and put some things together. He seemed very agitated. And everybody had left the meeting. Andy Young was there, Bernard Lee, my wife, myself, and Dr. King. His shoes were off, and he was just walking up and down and muttering to himself, and I said, "What's the matter, Martin?" He said, "I don't know. I'm troubled." I said, "About what?" He said, "You know, we fought long and hard for integration, as we should have. And I know we're going to get it. That's a fait accompli. But I tell you, Harry, I've come on a realization that really deeply troubles me." I said, "Well, what is it?" He said, "I've come to the realization that I think we may be integrating into a burning house." And that really threw me. Because my fantasy was that we would have the moral power and the force not only to change the political landscape but to change the moral landscape of this country as well. And if you change the moral landscape, you can come to a compassionate place about the poor, the disenfranchised, the lame, the old, all the things that we crush in this country, all the things that we find disposable: poor people, black people, homeless people, old people, crippled people, mentally ill people, all those things we want to kill off. The new politics.

So I tell you, yes, I feel that we have lost an awful lot. And we have done it in the name of integration. This is the first time in the history of our people in this country where we have no leader outside the system. The only one who speaks outside the system is Farrakhan. He's captured the hearts and the imaginations of millions of young black people because he's outside the system. The rest of us are in the system. All those young civil rights leaders, all those great leaders—whether it's Jesse Jackson or John Lewis—we're all in the system. We're in the Congress, we're in the government, and we're playing their game. We have to be re-elected. We have to aspire to the presidency. We are the chief of the army. We have all these titles, but we've lost our humanity, we've lost our vision, we've lost our culture. And how do we get back to it? I do not see our leaders coming together some place and creating the new Du Bois, the new Robeson, the new Martin King, the new Fanny Lou Hamer, the new Ella Baker.

CW: And that raises this issue of hope, you know. The great Eugene O'Neill, you might recall, when he arrived here in 1946 to put on his play *The Iceman Cometh*, was asked to comment on America. He said, "It's the best example of a country that exemplifies the question, What does it profit a man or woman to gain the world and lose its soul?" And there's a sense in which fifty years later, artists like yourself and Coltrane and Toni Morrison and others are trying to say, as the young people do, how do we keep it real? That is to say, how can we be realistic about what this nation is about and still sustain hope, acknowledging that we're up against so much? When I talk to young people these days, there's a sense in which they're in an anti-idealist mode and mood. They want to keep it real. And keeping it real means, in fact, understanding that the white supremacy you thought you could push back permeates every nook and cranny of this nation so deeply that you ought to wake up and recognize how deep it is.

That to me is a very serious challenge. If we were to take them back to '65, and, say, put black faces in high places, and think that somehow the problem was going to be solved, they'd say to us, Don't you realize how naive that is? And they don't say that in the form, We are victims. They're saying, We're going to get around that some way, but it's not going to be the way you think. We're going to get around it the way most American elites have, by hustling, by stepping outside the law, by shaping the law in our interest, and so forth. And people say, Oh, but that's rather downbeat talk, isn't it? That's not very hopeful. And the young people say, Well, the level of hope is based on the reality.

Now, what do we say back to them? Part of my response has to do with a certain kind of appeal to their moral sense. Part of it has to do with their connection to a tradition, from grandmother to grandfather to father to mother and so forth, that has told them that it is often better to be right and moral as opposed to being simply successful in the cheapest sense. And yet we all know that there must be some victories, some successes, if we're going to keep this tradition alive. If we're to keep alive the King legacy, the grand legacy of yourself, of Paul Robeson, and others, and be able to convince them that what we're talking about is real, what do we say? This is what I struggle with every day.

HB: One of the great advantages that I had when I grew up here under segregation and oppression was the fact that if I walked up and down Seventh Avenue long enough, I would bump into Du Bois, I would bump into Duke Ellington, I would bump into Paul Robeson—and hopefully Joe Lewis. When we walk up and down Harlem now, or the Harlems of America, I don't think the young people have any expectation of bumping into the icons and the heroes of the time. Maybe in a way they're lucky, considering

who those icons are. But it does say that we have so distanced ourselves from our communities in the pursuit of our living, and our
livelihood, and the other trophies that they offer, that we have, in
a way, alienated ourselves from ourselves.

The only thing we can act in is what they say we can act in. If
we try to bring really serious measures to bear, we will be dismissed from the boardrooms and the banks of America. If you
took the most powerful forces of black art in the world today, if
you took Toni Morrison as the writer, and August Wilson as the
cowriter, and you wrote the most definitive script on Toussaint
L'Ouverture and Henri Christophe in the struggle of Haiti
against the French, and you starred in it Danny Glover and Sid-
ney Poitier and Denzel Washington—the studio would tell you,
No deal. No deal. Why is it no deal? Too costly. Why is it too
costly? It's a period piece, and it would cost at least $50 or $60 or
$70 or $80 million to make it. And you must make pictures that
are bankable. But what do you consider to be a bankable picture?
Well, give us contemporary, modern, urban, youth-oriented
films. Make it filled with the energy of the day—which usually
means cocaine, shooting, violence. That they will buy.

And we have sat by, all of us—all of us have sat by—and
watched them run that scam on us to a point now where it's almost
irretrievable. We have got to find a way to get back to us, into our
environment, and hopefully in the reevaluation and the restruc-
turing of our communities, we can begin to impart new information that at least gives young people some choices. Right now they
have none. We don't know each other. We don't know anything
about each other.

We've got the money. Money isn't the problem. It's the distribution. If I said that I wanted to do this marvelous piece on black life, on black history, on black something, there's no place to put it because the distributor will not buy my picture. He says, "The three black people who will come to see your picture do not make up my weekend gross. I've got to have a picture that will cross the line, appeal to the larger community." The *larger community* always meaning *white*. And *white* means *nothing black*. And *nothing black* means you're voiceless, you're historyless, you're without. And I've watched I can't tell you how many of us sit out there hurting.

The truth of the matter is that we have to play the game on that level. If we do not seriously examine what the obstructions are to our freedom of expression, if we do not seriously analyze what stops art from black artists from reaching black people, we will have lost the vision to do anything. Because as long as we have to go through that other mechanism, we will never, ever—trust me!—ever be able to tell the truth about us and the world—to the world.

CW: I think that rage is an understandable and appropriate response to an absurd situation, namely, black people finding themselves in a situation of white supremacist power and hegemony. The question becomes, How do you channel the rage? Because it's going to come out. It's going to be manifest in some way. If it's manifest in a cowardly way, one not guided by political consciousness, it will be against self and those who look like you and often the most vulnerable within one's own community: women and children and so forth, physically and so on. Malcolm's great insight, among many—and Malcolm wasn't the only one; he learned it from both Elijah Muhammad and Marcus Garvey and others, and of course we got it also from other traditions, from the King legacy, from A. Philip Randolph, and others—was that we need to have some moral channels through which this rage can flow. And we have to have some targeting and direction for this rage. It has to reflect a broad moral vision, a sharp political analysis of wealth and power. But, most important, it's got to be backed up with courage.

HB: Absolutely.

CW: It's got to be backed up with follow-through. And when there's a paucity of courage, you can have the broadest vision and the most sophisticated analysis in the world, and it's still sounding brass and tinkling cymbals. Empty. If you don't have follow-through. And I think again this is where young people have so much to teach us. Because when they say, Make it real, in part they're saying they want to see a sermon, not hear one. They want an example. They want to be able to perceive in palpable concrete form how these channels will allow them to vent their rage and make sure that it will have an impact.

And I think we have to acknowledge that we're living in a moment in which it's not simply just that America's a profoundly decadent civilization, which it is. That point Eugene O'Neill made fifty years ago. Melville made it 150 years ago. It's also that right now right-wing forces are so deeply entrenched, it's hard to envision the kind of alternatives and curiosity you felt growing up in Harlem, finding those connections with progressive forces. That connection is no longer being made in black America. The apprenticeship for artists themselves has waned, so even the most creative and original ones no longer have any connection with the masters. Or they feel that the only way to make it is through a mainstream in which they become "exceptional Negroes," which distances them from other folk, and then they find themselves on display. And in the end that's empty, too. And they have high rates of suicide, depression, breakdown, collapse. All you do is go in corporate America and ask the Negroes there about their alcoholism, and their addictions, and so forth.

And what Malcolm, I think, was able to perceive is: Look, we're going to have to deal with black rage one way or another. Let's at least try to channel it.

HB: It seems to me that the only way that we can return to the kind of fire, the kind of courage that we had in the sixties is for there to be some analysis, some very precise and clear analysis, about how we happen to be in the condition we're in. I want to say something that might take it to a place that most people might not be able to embrace or deal with or think about. The presence of the Soviet Union and communism in the world at large was a huge, huge factor in the twentieth century. It became an umbrella for everybody who was ever touched with the desire for liberation, to feel that they had a place to go and a place where they might be able to find instruction or find an alliance to set out to do something else with their lives—including in the United States of America, where the labor movement, especially in the thirties, used many of the slogans that came out of the worker-socialist world: Workers of the world unite. We sang all the union songs. We found all the world, everybody, integrating and coming together, black and white. That wasn't anything new to the sixties. That started in the thirties with the CIO and Ireland and all those places.

We had a socialist ideology at one point that drove the twenti-

eth century. And there was a humanist relationship in the middle
of all that that people could embrace and relate to. That's gone.
So the world sits at the moment without an ideology, except the
ideology of monopoly, capital, and free enterprise. We need new
markets. We need to open banks. We need to put concrete everywhere. And what do they do in this new form? They can fire forty
thousand people all at once.

Now let me put a story to you: You take a white American who
has played the game according to the way America wanted it
played. He moved up the ladder and embraced all the corporate
institutions and all the American corporate ideals. Now one day
this young man who's going along in the family tradition there at
IBM, or there at Minnesota Mining, or wherever else, all of
a sudden he wakes up one day, leaving his suburban digs, getting on the train like he usually does to go down and do his
$100,000-, $150,000-a-year job. And somebody tells him, "Listen, you've just been laid off. Forty thousand of you have just been
laid off. The company must retool. It can't compete. The profits
for last year didn't show." He is stunned. He's been to Harvard.
He's got the degree. He's played the game. He goes to church.
He's done everything. And he's unemployed?! Like niggers?
How did it come to this?

Now, coupled with that, the fact that all of a sudden the health
care, and all the things that he spent money for, and put aside,
and the social security—it's all now in jeopardy. It's all going to
be lost. And in the midst of this panic, somebody steps in called
Newt Gingrich and says, "You know what the cause is? This country's gone wrong because of welfare. It's gone wrong because
there's too much crime. It's gone wrong—" And everything that

puts the blame at the doorstep of black people, poor people, the unemployed, mothers, unwed mothers, etc., etc., etc., who become the scapegoat for what is wrong with the system. And nobody speaks to the fact that the system is so seriously flawed that it can't do anything but destroy everything in its path. There's no way for unbridled monopoly capital to do anything but destroy. It must destroy. You can't keep producing more and more and more, and higher and bigger and better, and not destroy the rivers, destroy the seas, destroy the trees, and destroy one another. And in the midst of all this destruction, you raise your voice once to talk against the central capital and the banks and what they're doing to our planet, and you will find yourself somewhere in the Siberia of the New World.

To come to the point, we need to find a coalition that says that all these things have something in common. The destruction of the sea has something in common with the destruction of black people. The destruction of the trees has something to do with the destruction of Asian people. Everything you look at somehow has a corollary. And until we can come together and find someplace to analyze, and to assess how we deal with this, and set out to do it, we will forever be left to this thing that has us in this imbalance.

Everyone says, "What can we do?" One thing I would like to say to young people is simply, Do something. I put together We Are the World, and got my fellow artists to join in to help focus on the plight of distraught people in the continent of Africa, because it was something I could do. Because the world at large was doing nothing. And Africa was a place that was expendable for most people. And somehow we have to bring that concept to bear on the question of moral truth and moral responsibility. And I think as overwhelmed as everybody feels with mass death, millions, we can do something.

The other thing I would say to young people today is, Do not look on struggle as some harmful, negative thing. Struggle has great glory and great dignity and great power and great beauty. As a matter of fact, the more you discover through struggle, the purer you become. I think that if we could embrace struggle as a mandatory ingredient to ridding ourselves of this oppression, we'd find the most important tool through which we are going to be able to do it. So between doing something and doing it in struggle, I think you will have come on what could be a complete picture for the moment, besides knowledge. Because doing something, and doing it in struggle, has to have at its root knowledge and information, so that you're following some course that's designed. People who tell me, Well, just let me get mine, and I'll sit back and come back and help—it never works. The brother who said more people have been lost in luxury than lost in the war was telling the truth. Getting rich and getting successful and getting the swimming pool is as big a drug and as destructive as sniffing cocaine can be. Do something, and do it in struggle.

CW: My wife, Elleni, and I both have signs in our offices that say, "Never give up." And if there's one sentence that I would want to pass on, especially to the younger generation, it's, Never give up because there's joy in the struggle for compassion, the struggle for freedom. And because Grandmama did not live in vain. And as long as we can sustain that spirit of resistance, whether we can win tomorrow, or win further down the line, or maybe in the end not win the major Victory, capital V, but win small ones on the way, we should never give up. Because there's joy in being compassionate to others and loving others. And because the folk who came before who gave so much, they didn't do it for nothing. They didn't do it for nothing.

Bill Bradley

25 November 1996, Schomburg Center, New York

CORNEL WEST: My brother Clifton was talking to me the other night, and he said, "Brother Corn, things are falling apart. I'm convinced that there's just a few courageous, loving, good folk who're holding this whole mess together. And they're getting very tired." It's like the weary traveling in the last moments of Du Bois's *The Souls of Black Folks*, in the afterword. What happens when courage is on the decline in a culture, the very notion of sacrificing for something bigger than oneself?

BILL BRADLEY: Well, I do not think that you can underestimate the rippling effects of people with courage. Let me just take an example of the two individuals who successfully sued Texaco. If they hadn't stayed the course, this would never have come to the fore.

CW: That's right.

BB: They stayed the course. They did. They put their jobs, lives, etc. on the line. They stayed the course. They decided to make the complaint. It was a big media event. Big media event. Justifiably. Where are the ripples? Just today I was told about a major corporation in America where there were racist comments being sent on email within the company. And the president of that company discovered this and said, "Anyone who received and passed on that email is fired today." Now, not to say that the president of this company isn't a fine person who wouldn't have done that anyway. But I think that the courage of the two people from Texaco made a larger point, educated a larger generation of people. And this cannot be underestimated.

When the civil rights revolution was moving forward, there were a lot of people saying, What's the problem? until the problem was demonstrated. And once the problem had been demonstrated, to defend the status quo would have been to defend a system that was abhorrent to your own expressed values. That built a broad coalition to change the system. I think that this courage has ripples where people can step forward and say, We're part of the right side of history, and we're part of the answer dealing with this. We are not going to hide from this issue. That's the way you begin to regenerate some of the hope that came out of the civil rights revolution, even in the midst of very difficult circumstances for a lot of people.

When I do a town meeting in New Jersey, you get three or four hundred people sometimes. And they come in and say, "Well, what about affirmative action?!" And as soon as the question is asked, a switch has been turned on, the tension is up, people are anxious to see, well, what is this guy going to say about this? So I developed a little tactic in that setting—I say, "Affirmative action, okay. Well, before we get to affirmative action, let me just do a little poll here in the audience. How many people in the audience are for discrimination on the basis of race, gender, etc.? Raise your hand." Nobody is for discrimination, right?

So at least we've gotten that far. Then I say, "But let's assume there is discrimination. What do you do about it? Anybody know?" Well, no. Because most people in the audience have never thought about that question. What do you do about it? And then you say, "In America today, if you believe there could possibly be discrimination, there is no adequate remedy." What do you mean there's no adequate remedy? Then you take people through the passage of the 1964 Civil Rights Act, where the teeth were removed from this act against job discrimination. The most significant civil rights bill in the twentieth century, right? And Lyndon Johnson removed the teeth enabling the enforcement of the act against job discrimination.

That leads to the point where the only thing you have left is the Equal Employment Opportunity Commission, which also has no teeth, no ability to bring a case to a close, and ninety-seven thousand cases—half of which deal with minorities, African Americans. Or you can begin a civil rights proceeding, which sometimes takes five, six, seven years. It's pretty simple what we do here. What we have to do here is put some teeth in those laws. Give the Equal Employment Opportunity Commission a chance to bring things to closure. That way you say yes or no. But to do that, you've got to take a leap. And the leap is that you've got to give them the authority to do that. So if you elect somebody who's going to appoint toadies to the EEOC, well, that might present some problems. But if you have somebody who's committed to it, and you elect someone, then that person has a chance to make some changes.

So the idea is that you take the courage and you talk about it. You put it in a larger context. And you say, well, what specifically does that mean today in terms of change in policy in order to further the objective of no discrimination? Then you get to affirmative action.

CW: And what do they say then?

BB: Well, you know what they say. You've talked to them. They think that affirmative action is something that it isn't.

CW: Right. That's the problem. When they pucker up, they're thinking of black folk.

BB: And then you have to address the issue of white-skin privilege. The hardest thing to get across is that whites have race, too. If you ask that same group, well, how many of you who are white think you have white-skin privilege? They look at you—What? What is white-skin privilege? It is taken for granted, a kind of privilege that most African Americans or Latinos or Asian Americans can never take for granted. The point is that race is relevant to what happens to them in a particular context—renting an apartment, asking for a job or a promotion, or whatever. But that never reaches people.

So then you have to personalize it. And I personalize it by simply describing my first year with the New York Knicks. And I don't mean on the court. I mean off the court, when suddenly I was the recipient of a lot of offers for advertising. You know, would I like to be the corporate symbol for this, the corporate symbol for that, do this, do that? Those offers were not coming to my black teammates, even though some of them were better players than I was. Well, why is that? Well, it's because I had white-skin privilege.

CW: Now, if you had white sisters on the face of affirmative action, you'd get a more subtle, nuanced response to it, you see. But when you say *affirmative action*, they've got black folk in mind. And hence you have to be able—which you do masterfully—to provide some more complex characterization of it. Because in their mind it's black folk getting these special rights and special privileges. And so the challenge becomes, How do we get them to see not only that they've got to wrestle with their own racist sensibility but also that there are affirming principles that they're violating by thinking of it in that way? And what your story and analysis force them to do is deal with that tension. But not enough leaders actually want to do that.

Right now, we've got a Democratic Party that receives—what percentage of the black vote? Eighty-nine percent? And you've got black voting increasing at a time when voting among most other Americans is decreasing. But who did they vote for? Somebody who often doesn't give the story you just gave. Doesn't give the analysis you just gave.

As a politician by vocation, you have elected to actually wrestle with the issues that relate directly to these people of hope, people of African descent. What is it that led you to want to so substantively wrestle with the legacy of white supremacy in America?

BB: Well, I suppose to begin with the family I grew up in. I grew up in a small town, 3,492 people, on the banks of the Mississippi River in Missouri. It was a multiracial, multiethnic factory town. My mother was an energetic, church-going, civic-club-attending schoolteacher who poured all her interests into her only child, me. My father was what we'd term today disabled. He had arthritis of the lower spine—I never saw him throw a ball, tie his shoe, drive a car. But he made a living working in the local bank, and eventually he ran the local bank. A very tiny bank.

My mother always wanted me to be a success, and my father always wanted me to be a gentleman. Neither one of them wanted me to be a politician, you know. [*Laughter.*] I remember my father saying that the proudest moment in his life was that throughout the Great Depression in the bank he worked in, he never foreclosed on one home. And then he would say, "You can't tell a good credit risk by the color of someone's skin." Meaning that he judged people based on whether they paid back their loans, right? And in that sense I suppose there was that atmosphere. There was a religious atmosphere. I remember my sports experiences playing in Little League baseball. Our Little League was integrated in Missouri before the school system was. And I remember staying at some terrible hotel when we were playing the sectionals in Joplin, Missouri. And of course we were in that hotel because three of our players were African American. Little did I realize it at that time, but in retrospect, that's the case. So I came out of that background. And I went to college, where, for the first time, I became acquainted with history in a way that I hadn't been before. I remember a course in Civil War history with Martin Duberman that presented me with challenges of race that were deeper than those personal experiences that I had had.

And then, more important to your question, Why do I look at a career in public life with reference to African Americans? I think the first time it ever dawned on me that I wanted to be a United States senator was in 1964, between my junior and senior years in college, when I happened to be in the Senate chamber the night the 1964 Civil Rights Act passed. Which, as you know, is the act that desegregated public accommodations, hotels, etc. And I thought that night that something happened in that chamber that made America a better place for everybody: African Americans, white Americans, Latino Americans, Asian Americans. And the thought crystallized that maybe someday I could be in the United States Senate and help make America a better place.

I went on from there, of course, and went to Oxford for a couple of years. And then played with the Knicks for ten years. But that thought at that moment was one of the main reasons that I chose to run for the United States Senate in 1978. So when I got into office, to be true to who I am, not only to my background, my parents, my family, my origins, my values, but to the impulse to serve, I had to try to do things that other politicians might not try. And that's probably the answer to your question. Because I thought that there was a possibility of leadership across racial lines that wasn't always grasped by white politicians.

CW: On a very poignant personal note, you've been through a very tough period in terms of the deaths of your parents. And we know the Latin word *humanitas* comes from the word meaning "to bury." In many ways we are most human when we bury our loved ones. This is one of the reasons why during slavery one of the most dehumanizing features of slavery was that slaves were not allowed to bury their loved ones. Not just couldn't have guns, not just couldn't worship without white supervision. But when you can't bury your loved one, that's the ultimate act of dehumanization in a way. So there's a sense in which, when we impose some meaning on putting loved ones in the ground, we are most human. The tears flow, the heart opens, and so forth. And right now in your personal life you're wrestling with that most human of moments; and at the same time you're on your way home from the Senate for the last time, although you'll remain in public life in some way.

BB: Yes, I think that both are transitions. Both are times of the need for personal depth, understanding, and the capacity to adapt and redirect. I mean, the loss of a loved one, a parent in my case— both parents in the last two years—is a moment of change. Last weekend I spent in my childhood home in Missouri, and I'm convinced of a couple of things: One is that my mother kept everything. And the second is that a lot of my values really did start with them.

I also think that leaving the Senate is a time of transition and coming to terms. It's leaving the familiar for the unfamiliar. It's also a question of whether you change what you're doing because you know you can do it well or whether you're doing something different because you think you can have a bigger impact on things. Or a different impact. Or you want to challenge yourself in different ways. I'm leaving the Senate, but I'm not leaving public life. And one of the reasons that I'm leaving the Senate is because I want to try to lead in public issues outside the Senate.

CW: How do you wrestle with both fronts in terms of this definition of *hope*? Right after the national election, many of us are demoralized and depressed. We had an election that often denied, avoided, overlooked, or downplayed crucial issues. Very little talk about inner cities. Very little talk about levels of unemployment and underemployment. Very, very little talk about wealth inequality and income inequality. But before we get into that, is there a difference in your mind between hope and optimism?

BB: I think there is. I think that hope is a much deeper concept than is optimism. I think that optimism is something that's somewhat synthetic. It's something that comes out of the power of positive thinking. It's something that comes out of a culture where we believed in Horatio Alger. If you do a little bit better, you get a little bit better. I think optimism in some sense is sustaining in terms of moving people forward, a belief that tomorrow will be a little bit better than today. But it does not, in my view, compare to what hope is. Hope sustains in the darkest of hours. Hope goes to the core of the human personality, and our common humanity, and the belief that things can be better than they are. Hope is something that empowers a people, a nation, all humanity. Optimism is what gets us through to the next day in a narrower, more material sense.

CW: I would say that for the most part people of African descent have been people of hope, whereas most Americans have been people of optimism. Havel, the president of the Czech nation, says, "Optimism has to do with doing something because you're certain that things will get better. Hope has to do with being certain that what you're doing is just, regardless of whether things get better or not." And when we look at that, that hope and optimism, what is fascinating, I think, in your own life, as well as your own—I'm going to call it a vocation and calling rather than a profession and career. I think there are too many politicians who view it as a profession rather than as statespersons who really view it as a calling. And there's such a paucity of statespersons these days. But you have decided to actually wrestle with the issues that relate directly to these people of hope, people of African descent. What are the resources for hope?

Let me play the devil's advocate. What if someone were to say to you, "It seems as if the resources for hope in American culture are actually waning. The market-driven political system tends not to leave too much space for men and women of substance. The economic system is breaking records on Wall Street, but the suffering and the social misery, hidden and concealed, continue to grow. Families are shattered. The neighborhoods have become hoods. What are the resources of hope?" If we respect people enough to tell the truth, what does one say?

BB: I would remind people that we have been in circumstances similar in intensity before in America. That one of the things that is a uniquely American characteristic is the capacity of our political institutions to allow new generations to re-create themselves in the eyes of the ideals of the founders. And I would remind people of how things are different now than they were when the country was founded, when slavery ended, when the Industrial Revolution took place, when the country moved into the twentieth century and defeated fascism in World War II, when we created a middle class that was unique in the world.

I would remind them that there are today in this country a lot of things that are happening in our communities. They're led by people of integrity and values that nobody hears about. I remind them not to be dispirited by the cheapness that we see coming across the airwaves every day in the form of news or in the form of entertainment. But rather think of those people who are sustaining each other in communities across this country. I would remind them in particular that the six o'clock news credo—if it bleeds it leads, if it thinks it stinks—is not really where most people live their lives in America. I would remind them that good news is slow news and that bad news is explosive and fast news. I would remind them that there are people of character and talent in communities across this country who, if their stories were told, would give people quite a different impression of their prospects than the negative stories that we constantly hear on TV. Not to run away from problems in America. But to understand that we have a much deeper set of strengths than anybody imagines. I think 48 percent of the stories in the *New York Times* about young people are about violent young people. But are we really to believe that 48 percent of our kids are violent?

We need to begin to share the good news as well as draw back from the bad news and to recognize that the bad news is not as pervasive as it seems. At the same time, not run away from real problems. If people ask me, What's the major problem in America economically? I say, Inadequate economic growth, unfairly shared. You can't get everybody having a good job, working at growth levels of 1½–2 percent. And then whatever growth we have is unfairly shared. A disproportionate amount of it goes to people who are at the top, as opposed to the middle class or those who are in the lower middle class or the poor. And we can't run away from that. We can't run away from the fact that, when I left that small town in Missouri to come to New Jersey to go to college at Princeton, in St. Louis, Missouri, that year 13 percent of the kids born were born to single parents and that, in 1994, 67 percent of the kids born in St. Louis were born to single parents, 85 percent of African American kids. We can't run away from that.

We have to face those problems without allowing those issues to dispirit us.

CW: And then the question becomes, How then do we talk about resources of hope, given the Democratic Party moving to the right. Here're these black folk giving the vote, giving the vote, giving the vote, and what? Very little deliverance, it seems to me. What does one say in terms of this issue of hope, you see?

BB: Well, I think the first thing that you say is that one of the qualities of hope is that it's not a one-day show.

CW: Okay. That's right.

BB: That hope extends over time. And action that proceeds from hope means that if your choices are not the choices you'd like, you don't say, Well, I did my thing. I voted—once. And go home. You come back the next time and the next time, and you become a force that is clear in American politics. American politics today thrives on ambiguity. Maybe it's not different than other times, politicians trying to be everything to everybody. But the power in politics is clarity, I think. And if you have a constituency where there's a very clear point of view, then you have a very clear set of questions that you ask them if you want them to be accountable to your point of view. And either they measure up, or they don't. At the end of the day you see your choices, you make your calls as to which is the better person from the standpoint of your own circumstances. But it has to proceed, in my view, from a set of principles.

CW: That's the key. That's the key.

BB: Now let me illustrate in terms of the Million-Man March. The Million-Man March takes place. My counsel is African American, and he went down to the Mall. He came back, and he recounted, first, how it felt to be in the presence of such a large number of African American men who were committed to trying to change the lives of children by being there for them. And in that sense you could say that it's not a lot different than the Promise-Keepers, those largely white men who go fill football stadiums and promise to be good fathers to their children. Like with the Promise-Keepers, so with the Million-Man March, the proof will be in the pudding—whether people go back and actually do that.

When he was down there, he also had the following experience. This is America. It's the Million-Man March. People are selling hotdogs on the Mall. And there's this Korean American lady who's selling hotdogs. And one of the participants in the Million-Man March comes up to buy a hotdog. An African American man walks over, crosses his hands, and says, "No, no, no, Brother. Today you don't buy from her." And the guy goes away. Another guy comes. "No, no, no. Today, Brother, you don't buy from her." Goes away. The third guy comes up. He says, "No, no, no. Today, Brother, you don't buy from her." And the third guy, an African American, said, "What do you mean, I don't buy from her?" He said, "This is the Million-Man March. We're all together today. You don't buy from her." And the third guy said, "Look, the thing you're doing is the same thing that was done to us for x number of years. And I'm buying from her because I'm dedicated to the brotherhood of all peoples, seeing individuals as individuals. And so you can take that and go wherever you want. I'm buying my hotdog from her." He says that, he buys the hotdog from her, and he walks away. And so it makes you see that, well, what was the Million-Man March? The Million-

Man March was a million men, a million different individuals, some of whom went for this reason, others of whom went for that reason.

CW: Right, right.

BB: But the point is that there's a principle there. There's a basic respect for people's individuality and humanity and a commitment to that that is not going to be compromised, born out of an experience, life experience, where the pain and the suffering that came from it are not going to be transposed on someone else.

So what you do when you didn't win the election with the people you want is you maintain hope, you stay consistent over a long time period, you clarify what you feel is important for your constituency, you hold people accountable to the extent you can. And then you celebrate not only those who are national political leaders—senators, governors, presidents, congresspeople—but also those you know even better, who are people in the community who are doing the job every day simply because they'd be there whether they were getting any money for it or not. And you try to get them more assistance so that they can do the job. And I really think that that is where there's a tremendous amount of potential in our civil society, in our communities, in ways that need resources from a larger level but that are more creative and offer more hope than we'd imagine if we simply looked around the corner.

And what we need to do is to distill out of the things that work those things that are common. For example, you have a great idea in our great capitalist economy. You know, McDonald's, Starbucks, Banana Republic. You have a great idea, three years from now it's all over the country. If you know how to truly deal with kids who have drug problems, or you know how to mentor a kid who has no father, or you know how to reach a community by your presence, what happens? Well, you do it in that place for twenty years, thirty years. What we have to find is ways to take what is present in a successful effort beyond the unique individual and see if we can't move it to more places to have that spirit duplicated with resources behind it in a way that leads to some real transformation. Because what people, I think, not only African Americans but all Americans, believe is that the burden of proof is on those who are advocating change. Because change has been so long coming in terms of transformation.

But back to your question, which is, How do you get people who might not be interested to be interested? It seems to me that there are a couple of answers to that question. One is putting the morality out there. Not shying away from it. If you're your brother's keeper, you've got to walk your talk. You can't say one thing and do another. You can't profess to be a company that doesn't discriminate and then allow what happened at Texaco, for example, to go without any kind of remark or reaction. But morality isn't enough. I look at the opportunity that America has, in the post–cold war world, to lead by the power of our example. We are the only society that is sufficiently multiracial, multiethnic, to be a world society. And if we intend to lead the world by the power of the example of our pluralism, then we've got to do a better job here at home.

But if neither morality nor world leadership grabs you, then I would argue that you should try self-interest. Because by the year 2004, only 57 percent of the people who enter the workforce in America are going to be native-born white Americans. And that means that the economic future of the children of white Americans depends increasingly on the talents of nonwhite Americans. That is not ideology. That is demographics and basic economics. You cannot survive into the twenty-first century as a healthy, vibrant, growing economy if you have 30 percent of your people with high skills, 40 percent with low skills, and 30 percent with no skills. Can't do it. Therefore you have to be able to present this case to people. And you have to be able to pull back the racial lens through which they view issues such as poverty. There are thirty-six million people in poverty in America: ten million African American, twenty-six million non–African American, largely white Americans. But to the public, you see, when you say *poverty*—they say, Oh, well, that's a black issue.

CW: Absolutely right.

BB: But the fact is that there are sixteen million more white Americans in poverty than there are African Americans in poverty. Forget about percentages of the population. The point is, in raw numbers that's it. So if you pull back your racial lens and look at the facts, you have to do something if you're going to get everybody moving to a higher ground and let us all be able to move into the twenty-first century—with the prospect not only of realizing the ideals of our founders but also of realizing a better life for more of our people, whatever their race, color, ethnicity, gender, or sexual orientation.

In urban America I see three things that can happen: abandonment, encirclement, or transformation. *Abandonment* means that cities go the way of the small towns that lost their main factory. The town I grew up in was dominated by one factory, a glass factory, that employed three thousand people when

I was growing up. Now where the glass factory once was is a vacant lot, and nobody works. The company has gone. And by analogy, the cities could just be abandoned. People would have a suburban strategy. People would say, The cities, they're in decline. Who knows what's going on in there. We're going to abandon the cities. I don't think that this is going to happen. But the possibility of abandonment, through lack of attention and resources, is there.

Encirclement means essentially that we'll put up the walls of denial. We'll live in the suburbs and deny what goes on in the cities. And we think that those kind of walls, both psychological and real in terms of where we live our lives, will get us through. Which ultimately denies the interconnectedness of the whole economy and society. And therefore that's false.

Therefore transformation is the only hope. *Transformation* means people coming together. It means that you listen to the people in the midst of the turmoil before you formulate your policy, that out of the hopes and pains and sufferings and dreams of the people who are in the midst of the turmoil comes the policy that addresses their circumstances in the most tangible way possible. And I have a hunch that that means empowering those individuals that I call leaders of awareness that are already in communities. And empowering them in churches, synagogues, and mosques. Empowering them in community development corporations. Providing more resources for them to do what they do well. Distilling out of the good things the common qualities, and then being able to move those to other places. You cannot do that without more resources. You cannot do that without more investment. And you cannot do that without more accountability in our

educational systems. In this city you have an educational system
where 50 percent of the people who work for the Board of Education are in administration. I'm not saying that administrators
aren't good; what I'm saying is that the real action is in the
schools. I have a friend, a guy I played basketball against when I
was in college. He's a principal over in Brooklyn. When I passed
a bill that called for a day of concern about young people and gun
violence, I went to his school to try to call attention to that bill.
He told me stories of his work in which he was trying simply to
restore order every day.

So you have to work across the board here in order to make
change happen. And it has to become a priority. It has to become
a priority because to do otherwise would mean that America
couldn't live with itself morally, or in terms of world leadership,
or in terms of its own self-interest in the long run.

CW: Just one quick point, and that is that I think you simply have to
bring power and pressure to bear on behalf of those persons who
are the least advantaged. And that means that you have to come
up with forms of organizing and mobilizing that have an impact
on the powers that be. The very fact that we've had a 205 percent
increase in corporate profits since 1980, during a time of down-
sizing in which wages are stagnating and declining, shows that
working people have less power in the workplace. It's that lack of
power that allows profits to increase but wages to go down. In the
fifties and sixties, when profits also went up, wages went up. Because there was a social contract. You had unions; they represented 35 percent of the workforce. Today they represent 11 percent. Now of course unions aren't perfect, but no human being,

no human institution is perfect. But they're fundamental in terms of bringing some leverage for working people.

Similarly so in terms of the distribution within the corporations. We've witnessed a managerial bloat in bureaucracies in this society. You look at your universities—more and more bureaucrats and fewer professors. And their numbers are growing all the time: new program, new program, new program. Managerial bloat. You look at corporate America. Middle management, crypto-middle management, upper management, executive management. Managerial bloat. But who catches the most hell is the employees right below. And they're the ones who are bearing most of the cost of the present moment. And it's their kids who then go to schools that are disinvested with resources. It's their kids who have to deal with the violence. It's their kids who are often preyed on by trigger-happy police and so forth. And this is across color, even though it's disproportionately black and brown. So it's very much a political question.

BB: Unfortunately, I think that the media's focus on the sensational and the personal peccadillo does not create the space for high-quality public dialogue. I'm quite serious about that. It profoundly affects the way we view our prospects. It stunts our capacity for racial reconciliation, healing, and progress. In a context where race in America is much more than black and white, just look at what the media has focused on in the last year in America in terms of black-white relations. It's focused on three African American males: O. J. Simpson, Louis Farrakhan, and Colin Powell. One was ridiculed, one was demonized, and the other was idealized. If only that one were gone, hey, everything would be great. If only that one came, he'd solve it all for us. But with the media you can't control content. So the only way you help create dialogue is by holding people accountable. You have to get very personal with those who are making the decisions. Not unlike what happened at Texaco. What could happen at places like Time Warner. What is happening in other places where they begin to have their friends say to them, "You mean you're really putting that junk on TV?" Or, "You mean you really are not addressing the issue as you should?"

The point here is that nobody can do it for you. You have to do it for yourself. And that means that you have to be willing to put yourself on the line, and engage in a dialogue, and say some things that are uncomfortable for everybody in order to move things forward.

CW: What mechanisms do we have for accountability? There's a form of intellectual accountability where you attempt to tell the truth about the situation and you shape the climate of opinion. But then you also have to have organization on the ground level, so that you're not just talking but you can put talk into action. And that's what we don't have. We've got such low-level organization that even those persons who put forth a critique can't follow through on what they say because they have no way to affect voting. So the question becomes, How do we think of accountability across the board? Of course that's what democracy's about. It's about personal responsibility and social accountability in order to promote mutual respect.

So our challenge—I think this is a challenge that we've had from the very beginning—is how we as black people acknowledge our unique perspective on American democracy in order to deepen American democracy. Part of our problem, it seems to me, is that on the one hand we must have a sense of history that can't be sentimental. But on the other hand there's always the memory. And you can't wipe the memory clean because it's who and what you are; it's Grandmama and Granddaddy. So how do you shape that memory in such a way that you're open enough, democratic enough, experimental enough, improvisational enough, to know you've still got to move forward?

But America does not like memory when it comes to people of African descent. They want to wipe it clean. That's why we have no monument to the millions of slaves and victims of Jim Crow and Jane Crow. There's no monument for that because that shakes the foundation of America's self-understanding about itself.

I believe that there's no such thing as hope without an experience of despair. And all genuine hope has to go through the fire of despair. But despair is participatory. Pessimism is spectatorial. You can look, make an observation, and keep moving. Or you can be optimistic. You look at the evidence, spectatorial, external, keep moving. But when you're full of hope, you feel it in your soul. And when you're full of despair, you feel it in your soul. That's why black people have been a blues people. Because you don't understand the blues unless you've had the blues. And the blues helps you keep the blues at arm's length.

And so the question becomes, how do we bring that to bear with intellectual accountability, political accountability, economic accountability across the board, keeping our eyes on the poets among us? That's the beginning of an answer.

BB: Well, what I would say is, Don't start looking to the mountaintop before you act. Look at your neighbors. And try to organize your

neighbors in terms of giving recognition to the leaders of awareness. I think that the political organization that is waiting to be
called to action in this country is the political organization that
comes out of the institutions of civil society, where real people
are doing real things on the ground that flow from a set of principles. Do the work on the ground. Build your organization on the
ground. Try to give some credit to people of awareness—leaders
of awareness.

One of the things that I'm going to try to do in the next couple
of years is precisely that. One of the things I'm going to try to do
is to tell some good news. And one of the things I'm going to try
to do is let the light shine on the people who are, because of their
convictions and values, doing the job now, and nobody knows
about it. I think there are transformational leaders in America today in communities across this country.

So you have to really tie your judgment to your capacity for action. And that gets us to some of the things that Cornel said. To
the capacity to become a force. And while you want to make a
judgment as to how it affects the African American community,
you want to be able to get your vote out. And you want to be able
simultaneously to appeal across racial divisions.

I've committed my life to the assumption that it's possible. I
also believe that it will never happen if white politicians don't
take the risk of presenting the issue of race and discrimination.
And I believe that if the issue is presented fairly and openly, in
terms of some of the things I've talked about—morality, world
leadership, self-interest—and it is hammered home, there will
be more than a majority of white Americans who recognize the
importance of that kind of integration and common ground. And

I believe this enough to have committed my life to it, so I assume it's more than chopped liver.

Talking about race in this context is always more complex than any of us imagine. Is race primarily economic or social or cultural? Let me answer that by telling you a story about my aunt.

I had an aunt we called "Bub." Her husband worked in a lead factory forty years of his life. Was a wage earner in the clearest sense of the word. And I lived with them a part of the year, and I loved my aunt a lot. But my aunt had a major blind spot. And that was she didn't give African Americans a fair chance. And her language was sometimes abusive. And I would raise her consciousness, challenge her, reduce her to tears, walk out of the room, reason with her, plead with her. But it never seemed to totally change her language. She'd come to Knick games when we were on the road. We'd go out to dinner afterward. Inevitably there would be the comment that would make me get up from the table and say, "I can't take it. If you can't—"

The last time I saw my aunt was in 1988, late '88. She was living on a social security check in a two-room apartment in that small town in Missouri. Her husband had died years before. Her daughter had died. She was the last, and she was going to die shortly. So I went over to see her. And she said to me in the course of the conversation, "I'm sure glad you didn't run for president." And she always said, you know, "But you're still my baby," when I would raise questions. "Yeah, yeah, I see that. But you're still my baby, aren't you?" she would say. In this case she said, "I'm sure glad you didn't run for president." And I said, "Well, why is that?" She said, "Because if you'd have run for president, you would have selected Jesse Jackson as your vice-presidential can-

didate. And then those ———— would have killed you." And she
saw my reaction, and she said, "But you're still my baby, aren't
you?" And I left, and she passed away. And at the funeral, the
most eloquent testimony was offered in song by an African American woman who was her friend of many years, unbeknownst to
me.

It's always more complex than any of us imagine. And what we
thought was certain—that here was my aunt, whom I had pigeon-
holed for sure—wasn't quite that way. And I think, in a way, that
mystery in terms of human interaction has got to be the hole card
of hope.

CW: To talk about race is to force us to deal profoundly with our humanity. And hence we begin with hope and despair and *hu-
mando* and *humanitas* and so forth. It's just that in America, to
talk about humanity is to wrestle with, in part, this modern construct of race because it has had such weight and gravity in our
past and present. It will more than likely have gravity in our future if we don't have more Americans fusing, trying to create a
better world.

When I hear Brother Bill Bradley say, I stake my life on this,
that's serious business. Very serious business. It can make a difference that opens up a space so that other folk want to do the
same thing. But it's an open question. There's no guarantee of victory. That's why I'm not into winning in that cheap sense. History's not like that. The question is, Do you still have your integrity
after you struggle? That's winning. That's the question. Do you
still have a sense of who you are? Not perfection, but integrity.
And that's what that other America was about, you see. John
Brown said, "I can't stand to live in a country that treats black

children in this way. I'm going to do something that will upset some folks." But the point is that he took a stand. And Rosa Parks and all those Freedom Fighters in the sixties didn't conceive of winning in terms of some score. Or even some particular policy. They were making a choice about what kind of life they wanted to live. That's at the deepest level, and that's what blues people at our best have understood.

Young people need to have a stubborn memory of a tradition of struggle. And I don't mean just education. That's older people being in their lives who exemplify the struggle that they will remember. It's got to be concrete and palpable and touchable. So then the question becomes, How do we reconstruct our families and communities and churches and mosques and synagogues in such a way that we are more in the lives of young people as exemplars of the struggle that we know brought us as far as we are? Now, how do you do that? Well, one thing you do is try to seize the imagination of enough young people and ensure that they have enough visibility so that other young people can see that what they're doing is hip and cool. Because once it becomes hip to be a Freedom Fighter among young people, it's a new world. It's a new world.

Charlayne Hunter-Gault

7 May 1997, Cambridge, Massachusetts

CORNEL WEST: We'll start off with the fundamental question, What are the sources of our hope in this American darkness?

CHARLAYNE HUNTER-GAULT: Well, it's our history that has always been our source of hope, you know. From the words of "Lift Every Voice and Sing" that remind us that we've been brought out of the dark past and that the present is teaching us hope. Our history of survival and prosperity in the face of societally engineered obstacles. The fact that we have some of the most egregiously wrong and terrible conditions. In the sixties, when we marched and demonstrated and went to jail and died and went into schools, people forget that while massive numbers of people, young people, were involved, it was started by a critical mass that grew.

CW: Right, right.

CHG: And when people look around today and ask, What is this generation doing? they're looking at the headlines, they're looking at the TV, they're looking at those media institutions that, in effect, demonize young people, especially young minority people.

CW: That raises a question about the ways in which the negative images, the stereotypical images, in the mass media contribute to our loss of hope or our waning hope.

CHG: Well, I think that the mass media emphasize and exacerbate the negative. But what I was about to say is that in spite of the magnification of the negative and the aberrational and the bizarre and the sensational, I think that there's still a critical mass of young people out there who do give us hope. I see them, and I know you do all the time on college campuses. The kids who are being portrayed on television as predators are not the kids who are coming to see Cornel West lecture on a college campus or in a black community. Those are the kids who give us hope, who give me hope. And that is why I don't despair. Now, I do despair sometimes about our inability to reach into the psyche of people who still feel superior to black people, who still feel manipulative toward black people, and also into the psyche of black people who have allowed white people to make them feel as if they are second-class citizens. Those things I despair about. But at the same time I see enough on the positive side, the glass-half-full side, that I do not yet despair.

CW: I tell you, it's good to hear someone like you who does have a certain confidence and faith in much of the younger generation. You hear them trashed all the time.

CHG: I just am out there. You know, these people who are trashing the younger generation are like a lot of editors who sit in newsrooms and dream up things for reporters to do that are not based in reality. There is some sort of intellectual exercise that these editors go through, but they don't live there, ain't been there, don't know them, ain't done that. So they'll tell a reporter, Go out and tell us how bad things are in such and such a place. The good reporters either say right there on the spot, You've got the wrong idea about this, or accept the assignment, say nothing, and come back and tell them what they saw. Now, those who are ambitious and have no principles will go out and bring the editor back exactly what he or she asked for because they see that as the way to get ahead. But if you're going to come back with the truth, and the truth is different from what you were sent to pursue, you've got to bring your facts with you and be strong enough to convince that editor that the idea might have got you going but that it was wrong. And here is the truth. And it's tough. That's probably why you don't see more reporting of the positive side. It's because of the gatekeepers in our industry, the media, as well as in corporate America—

CW: And in the academy.

CHG: And in the academy and every other institution of this society that is still predominantly white and predominantly male. There's nothing wrong with being white; there's nothing wrong with being male. Some of my best friends are both. But if you are going to transmit images and portray people and have the power of the communications media—especially television, although print does its own share of negative imagery and portrayal—you've got to have some personal experience in order to be fair. And this is where diversity comes in—not as a Christian concept of being fair and all of that, but as a business principle. You have to have people who see things differently so that, in the intellectual mix, you can come out with a better representation of what you're dealing with, if you're honest. Some of these organizations do have black people in them and Hispanic people or gay people or women. But when those people try to present a different perspective, they're not listened to. They're just dismissed. But you can't dismiss somebody who insists on being heard.

CW: I know that's true.

CHG: So we've got to be convinced that there is a critical mass of young people out there who offer us hope for the future, but we can't just let them grow up like Topsy. We've got to help them out. And we've got to teach them. We've got to show them that our values helped us survive some tough battles. We've got to give them the suit of armor that the values of our parents and their parents gave us. And that suit of armor and the knowledge base, historical knowledge, will give them the strength to challenge and not back down. That's where the hope is. We can't just say, Okay, there they are, and they're good, and therefore we're going to have hope because of them. No! We've got to work on them.

CW: We've got to work with them.

CHG: That's right.

CW: But as an exemplary truth teller for years now in the very tough industry, the media industry, what has kept you going? How have you been able to keep your own armor intact?

CHG: Well, I've been challenged. There's no doubt about that. But I have just gone on, kept on keeping on. And then one day I had to really think about it. I was confronted by the question in part when I was writing my book. The muse must be a sister or a brother because the muse was saying to me, Write. And I wrote. And what came out was that I was able to overcome perhaps the greatest obstacle in my life to date. I was nineteen years old when Hamilton Holmes and I desegregated the University of Georgia. So when I was writing about that, I also was writing about my background. And while I started out to write an account of the desegregation of the University of Georgia, what it turned out to be was an account of this armor building. That armor, the layers, began when I was practically in the crib because it started with my mother, who couldn't get me to sleep at night when I was a little baby. She would start off in the rocking chair. You know they believed in nurturing. And she'd start off singing church songs and end up, after I hadn't gone to sleep for so long, singing the blues.

CW: Oh, Lord!

CHG: Well, you know, there it was. I was getting "Amazing Grace" and "Blessed Be the Tie That Binds" and "Jesus Loves Me" and all that essentially from birth— You know that there's this new research today that's saying that the brain begins to be a receptacle of knowledge from the moment of birth.

CW: Those first nine months are crucial.

CHG: And here is my mother, this little country girl living down there in Due West, South Carolina, and never been nowhere. She may have gone to Chicago for a couple of years, but basically her upbringing was Southern and small town. Unsophisticated. But instinctively she began to convey the stuff out of which values are transmitted. And then she sent me to my grandmother, who was the mother of my father the preacher, the wife of my grandfather the preacher, and she taught me Psalms. She taught me the Twenty-third Psalm when I would rather climb a tree and pick a mango out of it. But sometime during that day she would say, "Okay, time to learn your Bible first." And the most wonderful gift she gave me was "Yea, though I walk through the valley of the shadow of death, I will fear no evil. For Thou art with me, Thy rod and Thy staff, they comfort me. . . ." A child hearing that can actually envision the rod, especially if the grandma is dramatic.

CW: Oh, yeah.

CHG: So you think of it literally. And it's only later, when you get to be more sophisticated, that you learn to see the figurative meaning of it. But when I walked out of my dormitory room at nineteen years old into a cloud of tear gas that the state troopers had used to disperse the rioters who were trying at a minimum to force me off the campus and, ultimately, to kill me, it wasn't a festive situation. But I didn't walk out there as if I were heading into sudden death or harm. Because even at nineteen, I still had this literal vision of some figure walking beside me with a rod and a staff, a figure that was going to fight off any evil, like those out there. That mob was small potatoes compared to the armor I had with me.

CW: Sure.

CHG: So you can pass on values, and you can pass on stories that give young people the confidence in themselves and in their ability to overcome things. My father gave me another layer of armor when I was in—I don't even remember, but it had to be somewhere between the first and the fourth grade—he was serving in the army and away from us most of the time because they didn't have jet travel in those days. So if he was fighting in northern Italy or somewhere in Germany or overseas, he couldn't get home. It wasn't that often that I saw him. But he had left his values behind. And on those few occasions when he would come home, I wanted to please him because he always treated me with respect and a great deal of confidence. And so I saved up my report cards. I'd run to him, and I'd say, "Daddy, Daddy, Daddy! Here is my report card." I always had four As and a B+. And my father wouldn't even acknowledge the four As. He would go straight to the B+ and say, "Wait a minute. What is this B+?" Because he'd always told me I had a first-rate mind, for as long as I can remember. So when he would see the B+, he would say, "You know first-rate minds don't pull in B+. I want to see straight As on this card."

And that's armor building. That's armor building, confidence building. And there are so many stories like that from my childhood. My mother wouldn't hesitate to use corporal punishment when I misbehaved in church. And I did, a lot. But at the same time, my mother always treated me with respect. Always listened to what I had to say. She was confident enough in the teachings that she was exposing me to that she would listen to what I had to say. Often she would say to me, "Well, you'll have to make up your own mind on that." If it was something that she strongly disagreed with, she'd make that known, too. But she was a very soft-spoken person. And for the most part she let me make my own decisions. Like when I decided to be a journalist, there were hardly any black journalists anywhere in the mainstream media. I doubt if she'd ever even heard of any. But when I told her my plans, in the little country town I was in, she said, "Well, if that's what you want to do." Because she instinctively knew, because of the wisdom of the ages that flowed through her veins and brain, that fantasies and dreams propel ambition.

CW: Yes. Exactly.

CHG: She didn't say, "That ain't possible, we can't do that because we're black." As a result, it never occurred to me that I couldn't do things because I was black. So when I stepped out there, I felt prepared to take on the world. Although when you encounter reality, as prepared as you might be to take on the world, the world might not be ready for you.

CW: Oh, yeah! But now, in terms of what went into your decision to become a journalist, at what point did the issues of both race and gender begin to hit, so that even with your armor, you knew that this was going to be a battle?

CHG: It was not something I concentrated on. Both Hamilton Holmes and I came from this strong, proud Atlanta tradition of black higher learning. Education was paramount in the black family. My grandfather used to say to his children, and they passed it on to me: Education's going to be your salvation and liberation. So that was part of our consciousness, our psyches.

CW: Echoing in your mind and heart and soul.

CHG: Exactly. That thing, that armor. And so there was no question that we'd go to college; it was just a question of where. Hamilton decided to go to Morehouse because he loved Morehouse. Its students were excellent, full of achievement and pride. And I hadn't decided quite yet. When the opportunity presented itself to attend one of the white schools in the state, we said, Yeah, we'll take a look, because of the probability that they would have the specific kinds of courses that we needed that might not be available in black schools. But at that point, for us, the motivating factor was not the pioneering aspect or the history-making aspect. It was, Here's where we can go to become even better prepared. To continue this preparation for the ultimate contribution we were going to make to society. Hamilton felt all along that Morehouse had the quality of teaching of any of the white institutions. But because of Jim Crow and all of that, all the funds went to the white schools.

CW: Yes, yes.

CHG: The white schools had the best lab equipment. And no school in the South, certainly none in the state of Georgia, had a journalism school except the University of Georgia. It was for that reason that we were intrigued when the adult leaders came looking for a couple of what they called "squeaky clean kids" that the university couldn't challenge on moral or intellectual or educational grounds. So our interests coincided. But it was for the older people to think of the history-making aspects and the implications of trying to integrate a white school. Hamilton and I simply wanted to go to an institution where we could pursue our chosen careers.

And in fact, we were taken to one of the white schools in Atlanta. At that time Georgia State College was kind of like a community college, but we didn't know it. We'd never been exposed to college. We got down there, and both of us looked at the curriculum. And this goes to the point that I made at the very beginning about the hope for the future. Here we were seventeen and eighteen when we first started this. And the two of us looked at the curriculum of this white institution of higher learning and said, literally, "This isn't good enough."

We looked at that curriculum and said, "This will not do. Thank you, but no thank you." At which point the adults got very depressed because they thought they had lost this opportunity. Then Hamilton said, as we were standing on the front steps of the school, "I think we ought to go there," and he gestured in the direction north—which was Athens, where the mother ship was, the University of Georgia. And the adults just about died. Because on the one hand, they were despairing because they thought they'd lost it. And now that we were saying we wanted to go to the biggest of the white institutions, they didn't have any kind of capacity to help us—because they didn't know anybody in Athens. They knew they had a group of young black men in Atlanta who were organized and ready for action to protect us and all that. But they didn't have that structure in Athens.

CW: In Athens, yes.

CHG: So they were a little bit afraid. But they couldn't pass up that opportunity. So with that kind of faith that had brought us thus far on our way, they said, Okay. And then we began the process of applying, which took about a year and a half and finally ended up in court. But in the end, I won the decision. And it was based on the confidence that we had in what we had been given 100 percent by black people. It was that confidence, their insistence that although they didn't have the power to give us first-class citizenship, they had the power to give us a first-class sense of ourselves, and there it was. So I think that's part of our challenge that we have to pass on to these young people in whom we must invest our hope for the future.

CW: In your view, what are the major obstacles preventing us from passing this first-class sense of self to the younger generation?

CHG: I think that the biggest obstacle today is the larger society's continuing effort to make black people, and black young people in particular, feel inferior. To maintain that sense of inferiority in them so that they are not effectively challenged. And therefore what we have to do about it is to figure out ways to be sure that their armor gets built and that they help in the construction of it. You see, I think that all these other problems that confront society and black people and minority people and people who are different can be resolved by people with first-rate minds. But we've got to make sure we have them. And we cannot have first-rate minds if the larger society has so instilled in the psyches of the people that they are second class and inferior. That they cannot rise above it. I really do think that. I think that's more important than any other problem confronting us today.

You know, we often compare—and I think some of the comparison is appropriate and some isn't—ourselves and our experiences, particularly Jim Crow, to the apartheid situation in South Africa. To the extent that the state-enforced notion of inferiority was at work in South Africa, I think that comparison is accurate. As apartheid was coming to an end—it hadn't ended yet; the elections hadn't been held—there were people in this country who rose to Mandela's challenge to help South Africa, black South Africa, be ready. One of them was my husband. He organized the banks and some financial institutions in this country, principally New York, to bring over some of the South African middle-management blacks for six months. They called it the PDP, the Professional Development Program—wherein they worked at jobs comparable to those they held in South Africa, but in a different environment and a different system. You know, we've got racism in the United States, but still we've got progress. We've got black bankers, and we've got black decision makers in some of our institutions.

CW: Right.

CHG: But when I was in South Africa covering the election in '94, I was talking with one of them one day. This guy's name was Alan Mukoki. I said, "Tell me, Alan, what do you think was the greatest thing you got out of the PDP experience in the States?" He said, "Where it put my head. Until I got out of here and into a different environment, even though I had made it to the point where I was, which was not insignificant in that society, I still looked to the white people as being superior." For one thing, they were in the superior positions. And for another, there wasn't any organized consciousness raising. There were the demonstrations and all that, but they were aimed at bringing apartheid down. They weren't spending a whole lot of time working on people's heads other than to get them to liberation.

But this PDP experience gave him the confidence to elevate himself mentally to the station of first class. So when he got back, he was just in a different place. A place that said, "This is my place. I'm a part of this. I'm as much a part of this as anybody else. And therefore I am entitled to my say, and I'm entitled to have you listen and, where appropriate, act on it." And as I hear stories out of South Africa now, this is where I hear that challenge is. There are people in positions that they've never been in before, trying to function and keep the country going forward. To be sure, many of them need training and their skills sharpened and all that. But even if you have deficits—and many of them do—if you are convinced that you're as good as the next person regardless of the color of your skin, then you will be able to deal with those deficits in a way that isn't deleterious to your mental well-being.

CW: But do you think that, given the Million-Man March and the situation of so many black brothers, there is a difference in dealing with this particular issue between black men and black women?

CHG: You mean in their relationships? Because I think that's a straw man. I'm sure that slavery and all the other things that followed in its wake have had some deeply scarring psychological effects, and we've got to deal with those. But I think that it's really wrong to generalize too much about that. Because I see some brothers out here who are doing some amazing things. And I see some relationships between men and women out here that are wonderful. And when you compare us with the rest of the society, we're all in trouble. Everybody's relationships are in trouble.

CW: But what about in terms of how men and women think of themselves? I mean, some would argue that actually black women seem to be stronger and better able and more willing to deal with racism. Others will argue, Well, no, it really hits black women much harder because you've got both the patriarchy coming at you and the white supremacy coming at you.

CHG: Well, I think that if we speak too often in a negative way, when maybe the facts don't necessarily back it up, it becomes a self-fulfilling prophecy. You know, one of the myths is that there are more young black men in prison today than there are in college. It's a myth that we keep speaking—you've spoken it, I've spoken it, everybody who has an opportunity and the good fortune to speak before an audience has spoken it.

CW: Right.

CHG: But I was talking to Bill Gray the other day, the head of the United Negro College Fund, who said that a study had just been conducted that shows that just the opposite is true. And we just looked at him. The myth sounded good, and it sounded logical. We see all these brothers out here with nothing to do. And we see the images of them in the writ of TV—blown—large and demonic. So, yes. That myth makes sense. Yes. I see all these brothers out there, and they're going to jail. I've seen them on TV going to jail. Because on TV you don't see them going to college. You don't see them going to school. You don't see them working in really good jobs, wearing three-piece suits and carrying briefcases. Or holding their dignity as they empty the garbage.

CW: Yes, yes.

CHG: We need to speak that reality. Because I think that what gets into the common arena, into the lingua franca, you know, into the drum is effective. It has an effect. And I don't mean that you have to paint the world rosily.

CW: Right, right, right.

CHG: But you have to have some reality checks from time to time.

CW: Just to make sure that your myths don't take on a life of their own. I think that, given the quadrupling of the prison population in the last twenty years that is disproportionately black, and given the decline of the percentage of black men who are going to college, vis-à-vis other groups, one could say that there are some phenomena here that we've got to come to terms with.

CHG: No doubt about it. But who's going to do it if they're so depressed because everybody's in jail and killing people and robbing people and doing terrible things? You can't just look at things through a glass darkly and expect people to have any hope. You've got to say, Look, here are the problems that we face. Here's the objective situation. Here's one analysis, and here's another. Here's one set of facts, and here's another. Because facts do weird things, too.

CW: That's it.

CHG: I love to hear people talk about "true facts." I used to say that that was a redundancy. But, you know, nowadays—

CW: You can use facts any way you want.

CHG: Exactly. It's how you present things.

CW: That's right. That's right.

CHG: So if you say, Yeah, the prison population has doubled— There's a guy I know, a white-collar guy, who did some white-collar crime, and so he did some white-collar time in a white-collar prison. And he called one night, collect, and said, "I just have to tell you. Before I went into prison, all these sisters out there were asking me to help them find the men. Where were the men? Well, I found them. They're right here in this prison." They're sharp young black men, with good minds, who because of any number of circumstances and new laws, and that three-strikes-you're-out thing, have ended up in prison. So that's the real thing that we have to confront. You've got to give people hope. You don't confront problems if you feel hopeless.

CW: That's true.

CHG: You just sink and sink and sink.

CW: Where do you see black America in fifteen years, twenty years from now?

CHG: Oh, I'm a reporter. I'm not a visionary like you are.

CW: You're a visionary reporter.

CHG: I think that a lot is going to happen. I think that in fifteen, twenty years' time, it's going to be very difficult to talk about black America or white America. We're going to be talking about a global world. We may be doing that next year. We're already doing it. And we've already got young black people looking for opportunities outside this country.

CW: Hong Kong and Singapore.

CHG: I've just done a half-hour video aimed at interesting young black people, and in fact all minorities, in careers in international affairs—foreign service, government work. As long as we have a government, we're going to need people to work in it.

CW: Right, right.

CHG: This video looks at government work, which is traditional. But it also looks at some of the nontraditional things like the technology field, computers. All that's opening up. New areas for young people to pursue. And some of the traditional jobs. Business is no longer just local, it's global. And even if you work locally, your reach is likely to be global.

CW: That's right.

CHG: So that I think that you're going to see black America and white America become interconnected globally. Those who are in a position to do so, who can speak another language, or who make enough money so that when they go somewhere and need to speak another language and can't they can hire somebody to speak for them, are going to be all over the world. Already, there are more black students at Lincoln University speaking Chinese than there are speaking Swahili and Spanish, which you might think would be something that just naturally they might be inclined toward.

CW: Right, right.

CHG: They are speaking Chinese. And brothers are taking Japanese. Now, the Japanese market is a little funky right now. It may or may not bounce back. But the Asian area is an area of growth and possibility.

CW: We've got the resources.

CHG: But I think there are some real concerns. Technology has a good side and a dark side. There's a widening gap between rich and poor. As the top 20 percent get richer, the bottom 20 percent get poorer.

So I think that these are issues that we've got to look at, not just in terms of their capacity for delivering silver linings and opportunities, but for what we need to do to make that happen. Just as technology can help people, it can also widen that divide between the haves and the have-nots, between those with access to information and those without. And to have access to information, you've got to have access to technology, to computers, to the Internet. Yes, but these are all doable things. These are all things that can be done, provided you have the will. And we can develop the will if we can save the psyches of our young.

CW: We're right back to the point you were making before.

CHG: I tried to get there.

CW: This issue, the psychic will and courage.

CHG: I'll tell you this one final story about armor, and then I know that you've got to go and I've got to go. But I tell this story often, about this little poor black school I attended, which was typical of all of them in the South at the time. We didn't have any kind of resources. They had a little place downstairs, a snack bar, where you could get a pig-ear sandwich sometimes for lunch if you were lucky. The lady came with the pig ears that day. She probably made them at home, you know. There wasn't any assistance provided. And the school certainly didn't have any funds—I mean the books were the hand-me-downs from the white schools. Sometimes the pages were gone, sometimes the covers. It was pretty second class in terms of resources.

But every year they'd have a fund-raiser in which the whole community would get together. My uncle had a girlfriend named

Terry Lee. She was a beautician. And she would come. She was a school dropout, but she would come. The preachers would come. Everybody in the community came to participate in that fundraiser to raise our own money that the state should have been giving us, but they weren't. And there was a prize for the family that raised the most money for the students. And the year that I raised the most money—I must have been in the second or third grade. There's a picture of me, wearing this tiara. That night the prize was a Bulova watch and a diamond tiara. And they put that tiara on my head and pronounced me queen of the school. And I became so insufferable to my peers because every day I'd wear that crown, acting like a queen. They used to say, "Who does she think she is? Who does she think *she* is?" But, you know, I had decided that I was a queen.

So years later when I walked onto the campus of the University of Georgia and they were saying, "Nigger, go home!" I was looking around for the nigger. I mean, I knew who I was. I was a queen. So where was this nigger that they were all yelling at to go home? That was the kind of armor that came out of the community. Although my friends thought that I was insufferable, it's better to tolerate a little insufferability from someone who has a very high estimation of herself—

CW: That's right.

CHG: —than to have to endure what you go through when a child thinks of himself or herself as a victim. Because the two results are totally opposite, one basically benign and good, the other destructive and terrible.

CW: That's right, that's right.

CHG: You know, Seal has this song about how we were kings and queens and little black princes and princesses. And he talks about ". . . and future power people." You know who I mean? I think he's one of the most perceptive and talented writers of music on the scene today, especially his lyrics. His music is wonderful, but his lyrics are fabulous. Because that's where it is.

CW: That's where it is.

CHG: We've got to bring up a generation of young people who think of themselves as kings and queens and little black princes and princesses. Because when you think of yourself in that way, you carry yourself a certain way.

CW: A certain way. With confidence.

CHG: If you think of yourself as a victim, you go on down the street looking like a victim, with your head down instead of up. And that's what we've got to do. Have our young people walking around with their heads up and their eyes on the future.

CW: Oh, there it is right there.

The Reverend
Dr. James A. Forbes, Jr.,
and the Reverend
Dr. James M. Washington

18 December 1996, Riverside Church, New York

CORNEL WEST: We begin with the question, What do we mean by *spirituality*? Du Bois talked about it in terms of *strivings*, a term that he pulled from Goethe, and Goethe got it from Spinoza. But by *striving*, what did he mean? Is it struggle, courageous struggle—tempered by wisdom, lured by hope, motivated by compassion? What does that struggle have to do with people of African descent? How do we define *spirituality*?

JAMES FORBES: When I think of spirituality, I think of the systems of values and activities that provide meaning and strength for life, whether it is struggle or whether it is experienced in triumph. Whatever it is that, in a sense, holds the pieces together, the inner world and the outer world, both visible and invisible, from which I or some other person draws hope, strength, reason to persevere. And usually it involves both personal and private, but always social and more corporate, expressions.

JAMES WASHINGTON: I think of spirituality as a way of thinking and a way of being. It's an anchor that holds us together, individually and collectively, over against the experience of meaninglessness. I think that without positing meaninglessness as a dimension of life, perhaps it's hard to see what is the point of spirituality. And the way I try to frame it is to say that we are thrown into this world. We're pushed into it, then we spend all this time trying to gain some sense of self. And then you reach a point in your life where the body starts betraying you. It doesn't respond like it used to. And then you watch yourself deteriorate. I like the way Howard Thurman puts it. He says, "We're condemned to be observers of our own death." And it seems to me that through that experience there's always the threat of meaninglessness and the absurd. And spiritual practice urges us to try—or becomes a way, a central way, of trying—to cope with the meaning of life itself.

JF: I'm reminded that every human being is a researcher and that we are all researching with our lives the issue of whether, when the umbilical cord was severed, that was a friendly gesture or not. The way we live our lives is our report on our research. And your spirituality is your report on your research as to whether that was a fortuitous moment or the beginning of deep tragedy for us.

CW: Though in many ways, it seems, when we talk about spirituality, we're really talking about forms of darkness. How do we wrestle with death, despair, disappointment, dread, disease, all the various forms of darkness, that somehow seem to render us relatively impotent, helpless? It's very difficult to talk about spirituality in relation to darkness in America because America's supposed to be the land of sunshine, a forward-looking, rosy-cheeked, thin-lipped culture. But people of African descent in America have had to wrestle with the night side of America, which is part of the underside of the human condition as a whole. If it's not physical death, it's social death. If it's not social death, it's cultural degradation. If it's not cultural degradation, it's economic exploitation.

But some form of darkness with which these dark peoples have had to wrestle and then hone out some traditions of spirituality.

And one could argue that when the slaves first sung melodies on the ship, music seemed to be inexplicably linked to their survival—physical, psychic, spiritual, social, and so on. Do you think that when we're talking about spirituality in general, and black spirituality in particular, we're talking about darkness, the problem of evil?

JW: Of resistance to it, yes.

JF: Sometimes in the church the preacher tells the people, "Now just hum this. Now just hum this." You know. Hum it. And the preacher says, "The reason I'm asking you to hum it is because when you hum it, the devil don't know what you're saying." [*Laughter.*] It's like there is a knowledge. We know some things that the oppressing circumstances may not know. And musical expression, even without words, is a kind of investment in a different understanding than that out of which the oppression has come. I've seen this happen in public where there's a humiliation and the person feels that there is not strength enough to fight it head-on. And I think I've seen the mutterings of a subversive protest, just in humming. [*Hums a little tune.*] There's a whole lot in it, especially if you turn your head when you're doing it. [*Laughter.*]

CW: I've always thought that what sits at the very center of black spirituality is a distinctive effort to muster the courage to be. And it's so difficult to muster the courage to be. The forces of nonbeing and the threat of nonbeing are coming at you incessantly, and they have already left a whole host of scars and bruises and wounds. The white supremacies and male supremacies and vast economic inequalities and homophobias—all those ideologies and practices that lose sight of the humanity of you—creating these wounds and scars.

And yet somehow foremothers and forefathers had enough hope that they could muster the courage to be under such adverse circumstances. And I think that the music is probably the highest level of it. I think it's really something when you look at this darkest of centuries of the human adventure, the twentieth century, and you see black music, which is the greatest body of art in this ghastly century that's been preoccupied with the darkness, by these dark peoples, wrestling with precisely the thing most of America wants to deny, evade, and avoid: suffering, pain, misery, wounds, scars, bruises. But, you know, one wonders whether this tradition is going to make it into the twenty-first century healthy. Black spirituality is in profound crisis, I think. It's taking very different forms, and one wonders.

JW: Well, part of the reason for this is what you call the rise of the culture of consumption. And one of the things that goes with that market culture is the privileging of certain forms. That's why I said earlier that if you mean by *music* these things that people don't normally speak of, then I can see spirituality that way. When we had preachers like C. L. Franklin, who could take several different ways of delivering the word, that sort of utterance had music in it. You could hear it. I call it "Mississippi River culture." And all down through that river, from Chicago on down to the Delta, you hear the beat. And it's distinctive. You can almost divide up the United States into different river cultures. And each one has a distinctive beat of its own. Maybe it says something about our attempt to achieve visibility. Where we can be seen. You know, you send out a sound. It's like the terrible twos when one is raising a child. You notice you can give a child a pan, and he'll just beat it. In that beat you feel yourself, your presence.

And I think Ellison had the right metaphor, the invisible man. It's the experience of invisibility that often encourages and legitimizes the different forms of oppression that African American people have experienced. And how do you get visible? First of all, you feel your own self. And that founding makes you present. You know you're just there, whether they say you're there or not.

CW: I like that, though I think at the center of the black attempt to engage in various forms of courage to be is the quest for respect, which I think is most fundamental, and second, the quest for recognition. The quest to be recognized for who you are, not what the stereotype says, not what the image says, but for who you are, is a deep spiritual quest.

JF: The issue of recognition is made more difficult if you've been blessed with a family that made you think that you were actually the essence of sweetness, of grace. If you're in a family that tells you that you are in fact the offspring of the creative spirit that made the world and that there's none like you in all the earth, they tend to make you think like that. And so the mother who rocks that cradle gets a head start on shaping your sense of who you are. And then you run into a world that acts like it was not tutored at that school that you got your sense of consciousness from. They didn't go to that school. [*Laughter.*] Who do you believe is the measure of yourself, of your worth—that gentle voice that you heard and that hand that tucked you in, or the strident tones that question even your right to be?

CW: Inside black folks' souls there is this tension because the voices from the larger society are still heard. And the voices from behind the veil—of Mom, Dad, aunts, uncles, deaconess, cousins, Little League coaches, dance teachers, and so forth—those voices are still there. But they're in tension because they're often in stark contrast. And is it the case that with the weakening of black institutions, the weakening of black families, the weakening of the black civic infrastructure, the weakening of black churches, the crisis in black spirituality becomes more manifest?

We've got increasing suicide rates. Rate of suicide among young black men and women between eighteen and twenty-four has quadrupled in the last sixteen years. Unprecedented. Black folk always killed themselves less than any other group in America, even though they often had more reason to do so than other groups. No longer the case. How do we talk about this crisis in such a way that the richness of the tradition can continue to have some weight and gravity in the present? And I think it's not true just for young people.

JW: Was it Camus in the *Myth of Sisyphus* who talks about the problem of suicide? A great problem of the twentieth century. One of them, at least. But he develops that notion of absurd reasoning. When you live in a society that developed irrational forms of life—such as Jim Crow culture and even cold war culture—this is absurdity. And it seems to me that you've got to have a lot of courage to postulate the possibility of another way of looking at the world when the whole culture is caught up in what I would call a Disneyland that often does not allow for making distinctions between reality and fantasy.

The more we lose control—and we have lost control—over

the nurture system, how you raise a child, how you instill self-confidence, the more you limit the possibility of possibility. And the spiritual vision of whatever faith—whether it's Christian, Islamic, or anything else—is the chance that there's an alternative cosmology. That you don't have to be confined to what the world tells you is reality. And in that defiance alone, there is the possibility of at least reconceiving oneself. So you don't have a dime in your pocket, yet you can walk up the street like you're a rich person.

I wonder if in the days when you had black schools, black churches, black teachers, and when even if you had commerce in the wider culture, you could pretty much control the avenues in which that was going to run, there was at least some consistency and also some capacity to provide a societal context that was in resonance with what had been taught. So maybe the crisis today is an indication that breaking out of the ghetto introduced a second semester of life. First semester was in that more controlled environment. Now we are doing traffic in the whole world. And that requires the more advanced degree of making a case for how the world is.

As a religious leader, I always try to think that I would preach and that God would create the social conditions that would reinforce the truth of what I was trying to say. But no. So people who participate in a wider world, who are not in the mythmaking or the cosmology-lifting-up business, they are going to be in a very serious crisis. It is dangerous to live in a world in which you do not have the power to help shape the nature of the experiences in that world.

CW: It seems to me that the big difference, though, between present-day reality and the past is that even behind the veil of color, you had more of a neighborhood than a hood then. And this meant that you had flowing a certain kind of love, care, concern, and nurture behind that veil that allowed you to deal with the gang-sterism coming at you—namely, white America treating you like a dog. Organized deception, arbitrary power coming your way. Now, you've got hood as a kind of metaphor for America as a whole, as it undergoes gangsterization from the White House all the way down. And then we've also got hood-like conditions be-hind the veil in the black community.

Where do you go? What do you fall back on? We've got levels of isolation, loneliness, emptiness, and spiritual impoverishment, I think, in black America more so than we've ever seen before. I mean you could say that in the country as a whole. But that's what's frightening, it seems to me. It looks more like the world of Bertolt Brecht's *Mother Courage and Her Children*. It's just survival, getting over, hustling, making it, by any means, you see. And in such a situation talk about spirituality tends to be a mar-ginal affair. Something to keep a little distance from. You can't take it too seriously because it may not help you get over. It may not help you in your hustle. And like Willy Loman in *Death of a Salesman*—the dream is hollow. It's empty. Just like cotton candy. You bite down on it, there's nothing there.

Well, what do you do in such a situation? You have to talk about new ways of spirituality. We see this among our musicians these days. Some of them looking backward, of course. Some of them looking forward. New social movements in politics. New ways of activism that will try to remind people to reactive their subver-sive memory of years past when people did believe that there was an alternative to hustling. That's historical memory, historical connection. But can we pull it off? This is the question.

JF: I think we have to. But one way of doing it is to lessen the tension about the degree of the crisis. And by that I mean that we've got to begin to see that this is not a new problem and that what I would call the "problem of the presence of God" has been an enduring problem in African American history and culture. We just haven't paid attention to it. There is a chapter on God in Jay Saunders Redding's book *On Being a Negro in America*. And he wants to know why it is that we haven't paid much attention to the fact that God is a central figure in race relations, discussions, and life. He says, "Because different sides invoke God to legitimize different perspectives." And one could say that in African American history, especially within the religious community, one of the things that you see—if you begin to raise the question—is that God is a problem. God has a lot to account for.

And so you have those moments like the one in Daniel Paine's autobiography and recollection of seventy years where he says he was kicked out of his school in 1829 when they passed a law in South Carolina saying that free blacks could neither go to school nor teach school. And the first thing he did—and he records the form that he wrote—was to ask, "God, where are you?" We need to begin to see that God had to be a problem in the belly of the slave ship, which is the first ecumenical moment in the history of African American people, with all those people and all those languages and different cultural traditions forced together. And it's perhaps the spread of the myth of the American dream that has helped encourage many to believe that the pressure is less. But it's not less, it's just different.

CW: I think one of the great moments in the Million-Man March was in a speech by Minister Louis Farrakhan. He said, "We as a black people have the right to question God." Anybody remember that moment?

JF: I remember.

CW: The *New York Times* is not going to print that. But that was a very important moment because it was a focus on black spirituality, specifically for men. And Farrakhan stands in front of a million people, and millions on television, and says, "We as a people have the right to question God." And then he went on to say what? "Because we want to know why we suffer so. We want an answer." That goes with Psalm 44, when it seems God is asleep, trying to wake God up. How come you're sleeping, God? Let's get activated. Let's move. You know what I mean? Echoes of Jeremiah.

That's a fundamental question. That's not a question of ideology and politics—you can go one way or the other in relation to Brother Louis Farrakhan. You can have agreement or disagreement. But anybody who's honest about the plight and predicament of black people has to wrestle with the question he raised. But that's a very different spirit than the more upbeat spirit in '63 when Martin Luther King, Jr., assumed that God was on the side of black folks and black folks were on the move! I believe that there are many, many, many young people of all colors, but especially black and brown, who raise this same question Minister Louis Farrakhan raised. We certainly have a right to question God. Look at the prisons. Look at the levels of unemployment and underemployment. Look at these dilapidated schools and houses we have to deal with. We're raising the question, Is God in any way part of our new spirituality, or will we search for more secular forms of spirituality? Hip-hop, rap music, or whatever. And it's part of the tradition. In a way it's just an extension of the tradition you're talking about.

JF: One little contrast. You've got the March on Washington in '63, the twenty-eighth of August. You've got in September the bombing of the Sixteenth Street Baptist Church and those little children killed.

CW: Those poor little kids.

JF: That really shook everyone. Evil is a very choking thing. It's very real.

CW: That's very true.

JW: The dream is followed by the night. But you mentioned the secularization. Will we seek secular models to help us learn how to cope? I have a feeling that we are in an advanced stage of secularization. What used to be the African heritage of spirituality—a worldview in which the spirit had place, the spirit was in the trees, the spirit was in the stream, the spirit was in the community and the elders looking down—is vanishing, and so is the vitality that that vision gave us. Is there a relationship between the vanishing of the sense of the sacred at this point in our history and the withering away of some of the vitalities of the African American, our religious experience?

CW: Well, I think that it has declined. And I think that there's a direct link between what you're talking about and the levels of love and the levels of joy. I do believe that there's more joylessness in black life now than there was when I was growing up. I haven't done any critical investigation [*laughter*] and gone around and asked all the brothers and sisters, You feel less joy now than you used to? But from what I can see, there is a link between courage, love, and joy, a direct link. Which means that without the courage you aren't going to get political movement, you're not going to get social movement. There's going to be so much backstabbing, there's going to be so much pettiness, egos with the leaders, and so forth, that people are going to lose confidence in their leadership, lose confidence in each other. And that means that you can't organize or mobilize.

When you think of the institutions that the foremothers and forefathers organized and sustained, and then when you look at professional black people today and ask what institutions they have created and sustained, it's a joke. It's a joke! And it's partly because of levels of distrust. Before, in the past they bonded together against the odds. Which meant courage and love. And then they had more fun. They had more joy. Even though they're catching more hell. Now, I'm not romanticizing Jim Crow. I'm simply trying to keep track of this very strange experience of black folk making progress materially but finding joylessness at the end, more and more. And that means more rage, more anger, more aggression toward each other. And you can't create a movement out of that context without talking about that context and trying to change it.

Now you see, King, in a way, had presupposed a certain set of connections and webs of affection and support. But when we look to the Million-Man March, it's an attempt to reconstitute webs of affection. Now that's pretty elemental, isn't it? At least it is to me. And people say, How come you're not leading the revolution? How come he's not leading the march? How come he's not trying to burn down the White House? He's trying to put black love and black respect on the agenda again. Where is the love? You can't have a movement without the love. And I'm not talking about something sentimental. I'm talking about bonds of trust. And you don't want to get in the movement if you can't depend on anybody; you're out on a limb. So you need to put that on the agenda. That's a spiritual issue with political implications, in a way.

JF: Well, you know, the song they sing is "This joy I have, the world didn't give it to me. The world didn't give it, and the world can't take it away." We're back to the question of God. Because the song implies that God was giving you this joy and that nobody on earth could take it away. So is God in the joy-distributing business? How do you ask that question in a meaningful way? The world can't take it away, but you can give it to the world. And I think that's what has happened.

I see spirituality operating from a secular standpoint. I see it operating at the gambling table. I see it operating down in Wall Street. I see people expressing and practicing great faith in what the system will produce. And it's amazing how loyal people can be to a system that is obviously shafting them in more ways than one. And what I was thinking about when we began this discussion is that phrase in the Psalms, "How can we sing the Lord's song in a strange land?" Well, let me rephrase that a little bit and say, How can we sing the Lord's song in a familiar land, in a land that we've made our own? Because there is a distancing that has taken place. There's a surrendering of one's loyalty to God, in essence.

You can see this crisis. What Martin E. Marty would call a kind of global fundamentalism. I think that's a bad choice of words because what we're really talking about here is a clash between ancient and modern expressions of different faiths around the globe. And the crisis has to do with the immense power of the global market. Thomas Friedman the other day had a column in the *Times*. He was being playful, but he had a point. He said, "You can tell about the degree of friction in various countries based on whether or not they have a McDonald's"—whether or not that global market, in other words, has had an effect on these ancient cultures. And technology too. The faith traditions have to come to grips with how profoundly these things have changed the way the world is now. That's why I think the word *secularization* is not strong enough.

JW: Not strong enough, no. It's just idolatry. I would just use the language of idolatry.

JF: Precisely, precisely.

CW: I'll tell you another difference that I think is at work. That you can't talk about the courage to be without talking about the ultimate test, which is the courage to die for something bigger than you. You need to raise the question, How many folks today are really willing to die for something bigger than they are? How many black folks today are really willing to die for black freedom? It's an extreme test. But it's a very important question.

JW: Or a clear concept of what freedom is.

CW: Or what freedom is. Now, you've got a number of folk in America who are willing to die for the flag. That's interesting. Black folk willing to go to the Gulf. They don't know which gulf, Gulf of Mexico, Gulf— [*Laughter.*] Going to the Gulf. You're going to go? Yeah, I'm going to go. Which gulf? I don't know. What you going to do? Die. [*Laughter.*] Go to Harlem, go to the South Side of Chicago, and die for black freedom? Well, I've got to go to a party. I've got things I have to do.

Now again, we have a long history of different black people dying for a number of different things and talking about death in relation to courageous struggle. I know my grandmother had no fear of death. There was a sense in which she had spent so much time wrestling with how to live that she was then not just ready to die but had in some way conquered the fear of death. She also then, in her life, had a level of compassion and sacrifice and service that served as a model for those who came after—Dad and the others. And that's part of the tradition of struggle at work we're talking about. Fannie Lou Hamer and Martin King and others, they could take that for granted and build on it in a way that presently it's more and more difficult to do. See, I think about power, not joy. You only have joy because you have access to power.

And when it looks like God does not seem to have much power for some people—that's not where I am in terms of my own faith—I can see the point. And yet you can switch a button, and get different stations, and turn on the light—this is power. And you want a piece of that. Power is a very seductive thing.

JF: I think that you've got to the real issue. It's related to the addiction. Let me start talking about how we have been ensnared by the consumerist culture, how you can accept the surface things that speak of power, but they are not giving you the fulfillment that your soul is longing for, yet you're so addicted to them that you can't let that go. Then you have to deal with Thurman's notion of the depth and the darkness and then the luminous darkness.

And the decision you have to make is whether you assume that what you see floating on the surface is all that you're going to get out of life anyway, so get as much of it as you can get, and get sick from the emptiness since the promised fulfillment is not delivered. Or getting the intimation at least from the tradition or from somewhere that you'd rather let go of that and go down to the depths of despair.

But, as Thurman says, if you keep on going down into the depths, there is a luminosity that occurs. So if you decide, I ain't taking no wooden nickels, I'm not playing games and acting like I'm fulfilled at this level of things, then the courage to seek the rendezvous in the depths of reality is where the promise is coming from. But I'm addicted to the surface of things, and my advertising agency tells me that you can't eat just one of these potato chips; you need two and three, and then the real joy comes. Or you need a six-pack, and that's where it's going to come from, and on the first beer you're not going to get it, but the next one. . . . Or a nickel bag won't do, but if you can escalate. . . . Part of the issue of black spirituality today is that you can risk going cold turkey and that you're not going to die. Withdraw from the false promise of satisfaction.

JW: It seems to me that one of the functions of spirituality is to provide us privileged access to our own souls. What you're describing is a certain kind of labor. We don't try to engage in that. It requires a promise that you would overcome the seduction somehow and that you would get a different form of joy than the surface one. Maybe there is an anti-institutional spiritual tradition that is exposing the shallowness of some of the conclusions that we have made about our religious life. The dissent from the religious consensus may be the gift of spiritual critique.

CW: And that's very important. Because I think we have to make a distinction between institutional religion and forms of spirituality that are wrestling with the darkness. And the two are not always identical—by no stretch of the imagination. In fact, one could argue that it has been the relative failure of black churches that has contributed to the crisis of spirituality. Historically, they have served as such a rich source of alternatives to the seduction, but they have become more and more seduced themselves, so then where else do people go but to the other seductions, whatever they are, whatever forms of idolatry they are? For the middle classes it could be careers and professionalism, managerial status. It could be forms of addiction—alcoholism, sexual addictions, and so forth.

All these forms of stimulation have little to do with spiritual nourishment. But they are ways of killing time, passing time. Like Beckett's clowns in *Waiting for Godot*. Just keep things moving in routines that go from A to B and A to C and A to D. And that's not struggle. That's not striving the way Du Bois felt about it. That's just muddling through, just muddling through.

JF: We cannot defend ourselves against the seductions because those who are in charge know us better than we know ourselves. So we return to the whole question about a season of discovering ourselves again. We have to ask some fundamental questions. What really satisfies us? Do people really know what satisfies them? I don't mean a momentary titillation. But do people really know what gives them satisfaction, deep satisfaction? Or what gives us power? Do we know what activities we engage in that at the end most consistently give us power? If I watch a soap opera or even football this season, when I get through at the end of Sunday night, has it done anything other than allowed me to participate vicariously in a struggle, the meaning of which is not really clear?

What could I have been doing that would have left me more powerful? What kinds of relationships deposit a measure of human dignity, respect? How much do we choose for ourselves? I got in the mail yesterday a sweepstakes entry: "James Forbes has a chance to win one million dollars." I feel stupid tearing it up because just maybe— [*Laughter.*] It feels almost like a retreat from engagement. But maybe we have to humbly acknowledge that it might not be a bad thing for a season of the search for the satisfactions that are deep and lasting to be a part of the curriculum of spiritual communities.

JW: Yes. I think what we're missing here is humility. Most of these idols seduce us by encouraging us to be proud and arrogant. We create our little institutions, our little thought forms. We get arrogant and proud about it. And then we can begin to say, Oh, what does God have to do about this? We can be indifferent to it.

CW: I think this issue of humility is crucial. You can't have humility without confidence and security. If you're insecure, you're not going to be humble. In fact, it might make you sadomasochistic. You've got to get yourself together in order to be humble. You know Albert Murray has this wonderful characterization of Lester Young when he talks about "the earnestness of elegant self-togetherness." The earnestness of elegant self-togetherness. And you can say, Well, a whole lot of jazz musicians and preachers and folks you know do have that. But you don't have that if you're insecure, anxiety ridden, and therefore always worried about what others perceive you to be. You can't be humble. But if we could get that humility, which would call self-*righteousness* into question, then I think we could get the empathy. And I'll give you an example—

Look at the history of black comedy, and compare a genius like Richard Pryor with a number of the young brothers and sisters who try to make us laugh today. Very interesting. Because one of the things Richard Pryor had was the humility to laugh at himself. And his ability to put himself on the line, to have you laugh at him, enabled him to empathize enough to create other members of the black community whom we could laugh at. But he could keep track of their humanity while you were laughing at them. Nowadays, the assumption is that the comedian is the master and is talking about others to get you to laugh at them. So you don't sit in the front row anymore. [*Laughter.*] Because that's half the show right there. That's not all black comedians, but it's a very different spirit, a very different spirit.

Again, it's an index, a thermometer almost to measure the spirit of a group of people.

JW: I want to question, though, the way we're suggesting a decline in spirituality. I don't see decline. I see change. But it's been so rapid that we have not been able to index it.

I think that people believe in something. It's very difficult to sustain life without some belief or some faith. It's very hard. Maybe you believe in the needle, and you move from one shot to another. But why? Are you trying to anesthetize your pain? What's the nature of your pain? You find out what people believe in, what their faith is, then you'll know what their spiritual practice is. If you keep doing that sort of archaeology, spiritual archaeology, you can get at the root, the taproot, of what is troubling someone. I think that when we begin to see that, do that sort of diagnosis, we can begin to see a way out of this.

I think that we have the tools to recover hope if we see that people have not changed all that radically—they're just serving new gods. It's like Howard Thurman said: "The human being must yield the nerve center of his or her consent to something. Why not to God?"

Before we pronounce that we can't fix this, I'd need a little more evidence that we have tried to make it work. And by that I mean that I cannot get away from the biblical statement: "Seek ye first the people of God in His righteousness, and all these other things be added unto you." And it seems to me that what's said in that is that there is a center that has a mirror in it, a kind of cosmic center. If you look in that center, you'll get some clue as to who you are. But if you don't look into it, you'll never know, you'll never know. Of course, that's a theistic claim. There's no doubt about that. I can confess that. I confess it.

JF: I like it.

CW: The flip side of this is that if you deceive yourself, you're going to deceive others. If you're dishonest with yourself, you're going to be dishonest with others. And if you're lying to yourself, you're going to lie to other people, too. You've got to check yourself, look in the mirror, wrestle with your own sense, so that then you can allow the light to shine, and then people will see your ways and think that maybe you've got something going on.

JF: The question I wrestle with sometimes is, How much does God care about whether we pursue our interests as discrete ethnic groups as opposed to approaching them from the perspective of humanity? Anytime I go for humanity by way of abandoning the particularity of my own need or the needs of my community, I consider that to be a negative step. But in order to participate in the larger conversation, I embrace beginning where I am and then look to the larger configuration of humankind. That seems like a positive step. Now usually when I go to interfaith services, I say, I expect something unusual to happen here, and I do this from a Christian perspective because Jesus' last will and testament was: Lord, make them one. So that now that we are together across these lines of faith, I'd like to think that the Spirit's going to show up. Because Jesus wanted to make us one, make us all one group of Christians, make us all one family of humankind.

So my understanding of God as revealed through Jesus Christ is that God delights in and blesses situations where we come together with integrity. Coming together, being absorbed one by the other, is not integrity. God doesn't get any pleasure out of that, so far as I can see. But when people are willing to get real and deal with the structures that will facilitate community or destroy it—make it real like that—my experience is that the Holy Spirit's going to bring some joy, drop some joy. But that joy is not going to come until after the pain of discovering how hard it is to be real in a world that's made of tinsel.

CW: That's crucial. That's crucial. I'll give you a good example of this, though. You've got all this chattering about diversity these days. Everybody wants to be diverse, diverse, diverse. [*Laughter.*] Now on one level that's a wonderful thing. Because in the past they've been discriminatory, discriminatory, discriminatory. But if your diversity doesn't have any substance to it, if it doesn't have any integrity to it, if it's not genuine, then you're playing a trick on people. And what you're actually doing is allowing people to come in who don't want to deal with the issue that ought to be dealt with. And the worst thing you could do is to dispense that kind of cheap grace in the name of diversity so that people come in with smiles thinking they've done all that they can do, and the job hasn't even begun yet. You see what I mean?

That's why when we talk about black-white or black-brown and so forth, my view is this, that I've got to be humble as a Christian, which is a process. You can't make it without folks helping you out, and even then you're still a relative failure. Because as a Christian, I have a fidelity to failure. Because I know I'm a failure, you see. But I can be a good one if I love enough, sacrifice enough. So the question then becomes, Can you speak your truth, which is an imperfect truth, from your vantage point to preserve the integrity for any coming together that might take place? And I think that that's part of the tradition, you see. Fannie Lou Hamer wasn't trying to be diverse. She was speaking her truth. People who were interested came because she was a truth-teller. She knew that race and gender and sexual orientation and all these things were idols. She knew that. But she could speak her truth enough to say, What brings you here is the integrity, the compassion, what is human. But I'm not in a diversity program, a project trying to make anybody who comes feel good. Because you're not going to feel good. The darkness is not a place where things are going to be nice at all.

And in that sense then, if black folk can speak honestly enough, with vision enough, we don't have to worry about white brothers and sisters. John Brown wasn't in it for a diversity project. [*Laughter.*] He was just a for-real white brother. He went where there was integrity, where something was going on. Miles Horton wasn't like that, Anne Braden's not like that. So it's not going to be a question of being inclusive and diverse and hoping you don't hurt people's feelings. It's going to be honest, candid. It's saying, I love you enough to acknowledge that you are like me. You're a relative failure. I love you anyway. Let's try to do something together. And I think that once we reach that level, we don't really have to worry a lot about some of the other versions of multiculturalism where everybody's coming in feeling as if somehow they have to have their feelings on the table, as opposed to being taken seriously. That's a very different kind of thing. I'm sorry to spend a lot of time on it.

JW: I agree with what both of you have said. I think that one of the things that we've got to factor in here—not that you haven't, but I just want to make it more explicit—is that when you have a hegemony, when you have what is constituted as white supremacy, you have a model of what is the legitimate self and what is not, collectively and individually. If you try to be yourself in a situation like that, there are penalties that you suffer.

CW: That's right. That's true.

JW: And when you have that situation, I think it's compounded—especially for African Americans—by what Herskovits calls "the myth of the Negro past." Because the claim has been that they don't have a past. They don't have a past, they don't have a history. It was a new idea in 1972, when John Blassingame put out his book *Slave Community,* that the slaves actually had a community. It was revolutionary in that sense. So the people who are black often don't know who they have been. And the people black folk are trying to relate to certainly don't have a sense. So how can you have the kind of integrity that you're talking about when there is this—for lack of a better word—amnesia? But it's not amnesia in a clinical sense. There have been traumas. There have been hurts. And sometimes we mismanage the hurt by denying that it took place. And until we revisit the hurt, we will not be able to get back those pieces of who we have been. They're buried, and we're in denial of that.

JF: And if you have a bad memory, you're really messed up.

JW: It sounds like race matters to me, so I want to raise this issue. George Kelsey, in *Racism and the Christian Understanding of Man*, talks about the fact that if you allow race to become as important in America as it has tended to be, you are engaged in an idolatrous situation, which has to be a spiritual problem. That people who are locked into the prerogatives, privileges, of race cannot be a part of a healthy community. What is this thing called *race* good for from a spiritual perspective?

CW: I think that significant numbers of black folk have used race to actually produce some of the grandest spiritual and cultural achievements in this nation. There's no "A Love Supreme" by John Coltrane without race. But what did he do with it? He asked us to keep track of race in terms of its evils. It can be an idol, too. He accented the positive side of race in terms of creating a community, creating new ways of looking at the world. "A Love Supreme" is ecumenical, universal, international, cosmopolitan, transnational, across the board. But it is also thoroughly rooted in the black community, the black musical tradition, and so forth.

So in that sense I think there are certain geniuses in the black community who have used race for good. It's good in relation to something bigger than themselves, something bigger than race—the human race and of course God.

JW: That's correct. If we work hard enough on ourselves, we can constitute the beginnings of what King called "the beloved community." And I think that in the end that's what we're after. But there's a whole lot of work to be done.

Wynton Marsalis

14 October 1996, Schomburg Center, New York

CORNEL WEST: How do we talk about jazz? Let me begin by asking Brother Wynton, How would you define a blues sensibility or even a blues philosophy? Do you think there's such a thing? And if so, how would you define it?

WYNTON MARSALIS: Well, I think that the blues is many things. For instance, on a most basic level, it's the sound. The sound of somebody's voice. The blues is a down-home sound. It makes you feel good, like you're down home, which is always where you want to be. You know, a friend of mine is a policeman. He says it shocked him that every time they put the dogs on people and the dogs would get them, they start crying for their mama. So that's the blues. [*Laughter.*] The blues is the sound of their mother's voice. That's the blues.

The blues is a form in music. The basic blues is a twelve-bar form, which is like the twelve inches of a ruler, the twelve months of the year, a dozen eggs. You know, we have a lot of twelves. Twelve numbers on a clock. The blues is also a conception of harmony. In music when you put two notes together, that's harmony. And the blues harmonies—there are no rules about it, but it is a dissonance and a consonance. If you hear somebody sing some blues, he might say:

> The woman I love,
> Left with my best friend;
> Some joker got lucky,
> He stole his woman back again.

So now when you say "stole his woman back again," that kind of sound is dissonant and it's consonant at the same time. That's why it feels good. "Stole his woman back again." You say, yeah, okay. Mmmm. So that's the blues. The blues is conflict and resolution. We hear blues melodies all the time. And the blues is not just the melody, but it's the sound of it.

The blues is a series of different tempers, like growls, and cries, and shouts. Because that's what the people would do down home. You'd hear them playing the banjo, or they're working in the fields, or even if they're singing in church. One of the great dichotomies, the thing that's interesting about the blues, is how you have Mahalia Jackson and Florence Bessie Smith. You know, Duke Ellington had to beg Mahalia Jackson for about twenty-five years to sing with his band because she thought there wasn't something in it that was religious and spiritual. But when they asked, "Well, who do you listen to?" she said, "I listen to Bessie Smith." So the blues has that type of quality; it's profane and spiritual.

So with the blues, we have a bunch of different sounds. If you're a trumpet player, you can play the "Brandenburg Concerto," or the Haydn Trumpet Concerto, or even the great cornet solos of Herbert L. Clark. And you will never get to the type of sounds that you have in the blues.

CW: It seems that you're saying in part that the blues is a form of affirmation in the midst of the darkness and the thunder.

WM: Right. The greatest book written on the blues is by a man who lives right around the corner here on 132d Street, Albert Murray. And the book is entitled *Stomping the Blues*. 1976, I think, it was published.

CW: Yes, that is a classic. But why is it that people of African descent in the New World played that way, more so than others? We're not talking about better or worse at this point. It's just different. What was going on among these folks to lead them to produce those kinds of notes?

WM: Well, first you have to realize that the people didn't want to produce jazz. You see, they wanted to be African, or they wanted to be Creole, or they wanted to be white. Jazz music came about because the Creoles had to fight for jobs with the black musicians. Now, if you ever knew a Creole, the Creoles do not think that they are black. Not all, but most.

CW: I know.

WM: So you also had the white musicians who were always very interested in learning and playing different styles of music. And you also had a system of teaching and education where all the different musicians would get together. Because, you see, even in the era of segregation, the musician always was like a little different class. Because if you're a trumpet player, and you hear people playing something you can't play, the color of their skin becomes secondary to what they're playing, and you couldn't segregate the airwaves.

You know before 1900 after the Robert Charles race riots in

New Orleans, there was an astonishing amount of integration among people. And I always like to say that jazz music came about as a result of integration—some forced—but a lot of integration. "Jelly Roll" Morton said that in the New Orleans of that time, you had all kinds of people—Italian, French, Spanish, different groups of Native Americans (they said "Indians"), people from the Caribbean. You know, a lot of people together.

The fact that the Creole musicians were forced to vie for jobs with the black musicians meant that there was a coming together of a certain type of information. Like from the European school of training that the Creole musician had and the type of hollering and shouting that took place in the church. Now, the Creole musicians said that that music was beneath them. That's just a bunch of animal sounds. But when they needed to get a job, they said, Well.... [*Laughter.*] Suddenly the low has become high. And for the dark-skinned musicians, the question for them was, How can we address this sophistication? And they strove to address the sophistication, the technical virtuosity, of the Creole musicians. And the Creole musicians strove to get the type of sounds and nuances that those musicians got.

Another thing is that whenever you're left out of something, your feeling for it is always greater because you're excluded from it. I learned this from Marcus Roberts, who's blind, who was on the road with me. He never could see, so seeing meant something to him. He always used to tell me, "Man, you know, people only use 20 percent of their vision." He said, "Look around, man." I would joke, "Well, man, if you looked around, you'd be glad you couldn't see." But I learned a lot from what he said, from what a lot of the musicians said, because they were excluded from participating in the United States of America on a certain level. That's what they wanted to do. They wanted that.

There's a certain soul and warmth that these people had, you know. They were trying to figure out how to get along and deal with each other. And that's what jazz music is; that's why you have this type of aesthetic coming from that generation of people. Because first the people were not racist. You can read a thousand interviews with the older jazz musicians, and you will not hear one drop of vitriol. Now, in the seventies, I used to think that was tomming. But that wasn't in them as men. That's not what was on their minds. When Bix Beiderbecke heard Louis Armstrong, he just looked around and said, "What? What is that coming out of his horn? And how can I play it?" *Not*, "Boy, sure must be something to be black." It was, "How can I play that?" And Louis Armstrong, I'm sure he felt that when he heard King Oliver play with Manuel Perez, Bob Johnson, and Freddie Keppert. Let alone the cornet soloists, who were almost all white, with the exception of a cornet soloist in the early 1900s, William Johnson, I think, who went to England and played for the queen. There was a great tradition of cornetists like Herbert Clark, and Jules Levy. That was in the air. So that type of virtuosity is reflected in Louis Armstrong's playing. And if it weren't in there, then he wouldn't be Louis Armstrong.

So that's really where jazz music is coming from. And that's why I never try to separate the music from the reality of our situation, especially of the musician. Because that's not the truth of the music. You know, a lot of black musicians in the thirties had German band instructors. Now, the German band instructors weren't teaching them anything about swing, you know.

CW: They knew how to swing already.

WM: Well, they weren't learning from any German. [*Laughter.*] But they weren't sitting in their lessons asking, Can you swing, though? They were saying, Now, how can I hit this high C? Or, How can I learn all my major scales? Or, What about slurring? Those are things that musicians think about. Music, our music, has always been very integrated. For example, George Gershwin studied with Fats Waller. He was intimately familiar with the style, and the musicians enjoyed playing his music. And Coleman Hawkins studied the cello. I'm talking way back. So our music has always been people trying to figure out, what is this, what is that. Beethoven, Bach's music. Not out of prejudice or ignorance. That came in later, much later. And that's why the level of the music declined.

CW: Well, we're going to deal with that. The great Duke Ellington once said, "Jazz is freedom." And you once defined jazz in part as "those who are willing to work hard enough to be free and then to use their freedom to help other people get their freedom, like Harriet Tubman, for example." This is just a direct quote from your wise words. Is it the case that one of the reasons, with the blues backdrop, that jazz does emerge when it does, given this amalgamation, given this cross-cultural fertilization, is because of this preoccupation with freedom, with this open-endedness, this willingness to experiment, this willingness to be fluid and flexible, and to allow what's on the outside to penetrate, and also to be willing to embrace selectively and critically what's on the outside? And if that's so, then does that say something, at the existential and artistic level, about jazz musicians? Because I've always argued that jazz musicians are the freest black people in

America. And what I mean by that is that they are free enough in their hearts and minds and souls to be themselves.

I think that the courage to be is the most difficult thing for any human being. And it's painful. It hurts. It creates discomfort. And if people have the audacity to view themselves as a jazz musician, that means they're free. Which means they're going to be digging deep into the abyss of themselves. And then producing a sound that will both allow people to feel good and also create both a comfort and a discomfort because you want to create enough comfort to bring them in but enough discomfort to solicit their struggle so that they start struggling within themselves to be free. Now, if that's true, the question becomes, What are the ways in which jazz becomes, not just a signifier of this art form, but a barometer of the degree of freedom wrestling that's taking place in black America and in America—on the globe in many ways?

WM: Well, once again, it depends on where we want to pick it up. You want to talk about some of the first jazz musicians? Some of the second generation, third? Each generation is different. It's like, if you've got to go out and work, and you make a pile of money, and you give it to me, and I didn't have to work for it, my attitude toward that work is going to be different from yours.

CW: Oh, yeah.

WM: So we have to remember that for a people who had come from a legacy of slavery, just to be known as Louis Armstrong was something great. Instead of, well, "that nigger over there" or "say, boy!" We have to remember. I always have to think myself that my father grew up under segregation. He was twenty-six years old by the time he could sit at the front of a streetcar.

But the thing about the jazz musician has always been a certain persona. And not just the blacks. You've always got to remember, now, something that's not talked about too much. Let's say you were a white person in 1926, '27, and you're playing jazz. You go back to your family, they're going to ask you, "Why you want to play them niggers' music? That's what you're going to do?" You come from a family where they've been lawyers or whatever. They're not going to be saying, "Wow! Great! Louis Armstrong? Yeah, baby!" [*Laughter.*] I mean, you had musicians like Bunny Berigan, who would be saying, "All you need to be a musician is a toothbrush and a picture of Louis Armstrong." And Bunny Berigan was white. You had a certain feeling among the musicians— and it took me a long time to understand, coming from a seventies perspective. When I'm around musicians like Benny Carter and Dizzy Gillespie, they say, "Son, this music is about this." And the feeling of these men is not one of "we're African Americans." It's "we're human beings."

I did interviews with a lot of musicians for this radio show called "Making the Music" that was on NPR. And they'd all say, "This music is about love." And when we talk about "freedom," you have on the one hand the freedom to be yourself. But now once you get down there, you have to feel that you've found something that's worth somebody else hearing. Which is what you were talking about, that conflict you have. On the one hand it's a conflict that someone else can relate to, you see. "Man, I went through that same thing." But on the other hand, you've got to find something. Like Picasso said once, "I do not seek. I find." So if you don't find anything when you get down there, then you'd better have a good agent or a good record company. Because I came to jazz not through the music but more through the musicians, the jazz musician always seemed to me very deep in his soul, like my father.

CW: That's true.

WM: We'd be in the barbershop—and it was called Parker's Barbershop—and Parker would be up in there talking, and you couldn't say anything when you were young. If you said something, everybody would just be quiet for a little while. But my daddy and them would come in there, and whenever they'd start talking, all the other brothers in the shop would be like, "Well, you know, Ellis is a musician. Now, you know, he's been around the world. We can't mess with him." I mean the musicians just had a certain thing about them, a feeling, just a vibration. And they weren't judgmental.

CW: In a way that definition of *soulful* is similar to your definition of *blues*, down-home sophistication, down-home elegance, down-home excellence.

WM: Yeah. . . .

CW: And when you look at it in that way, then again it takes us to the issue that I'm deeply concerned about in relation to hope and despair, which is courage and maturity. Because there's no maturity without wrestling with oneself. But the maturity itself is a perennial process because you're continually wrestling with yourself. When you see a jazz musician, you say, Now there's somebody who's involved in some soul wrestling. Now what is soul wrestling? Well, in part—and here we can even invoke John Keats, the great English poet of the nineteenth century—we say, well, soul wrestling has to do with when you have enough courage to wrestle with yourself in the midst of doubt, mystery, and uncertainty without any irritable reaching after reason or fact. You're just out there dangling: remaking yourself, reinventing yourself; finding your voice, as it were. And each jazz musician has to find his or her voice.

But why is it that the two towering figures—and you can see whether we agree or not—the two towering figures in jazz are in some way the originating figures? Armstrong and Ellington. Would you agree with that?

WM: Yes.

CW: And if so, why is it that you start off with these two towering figures, then you've got this kind of caravan of geniuses, and then you get a little slow drop-off? Why is it that at the very beginning you get these two towering figures?

WM: Because whenever the original impetus, that original feeling, something comes into existence, it has that spark in it. It's new. It's like the first time you tasted a banana. Damn, what was that? I was eating with a guy once who was allergic to shrimp. He never ate a shrimp. So he was eating these things. "Man, what is this? It's great!" I said, "That's a shrimp." [*Laughter.*] He said, "Oh, no, a shrimp!" But when the thing is first created, it has the original impetus, it has a drive to it already. Just boom! And then it takes an effort to maintain it. And as it continues, it takes even more effort. Civilization is effort, is effort. The effort is not just going to take care of itself.

I saw my father struggle with that his entire life, and he had a hard life. My brother and I used to laugh. We were like fourteen, and I couldn't play. You know, I was thirteen. We played in a funk band called the Creators. We had on all kinds of satin and strobe lights, stuff blowing up. Man, we'd go to a gig, there'd be two thousand people easy at the top of this big warehouse. Packed with people jamming. We'd go to see my daddy play, there'd be ten people.

CW: Oh, yeah.

WM: My daddy'd make a gig $40, $35. He's got six children. My brother and I play a gig, a bill and a half, $125. We'd be like, "Man, we make more money than you. And we can't even play." [*Laughter.*] And he'd say, "Yeah, boy. That's something, ain't it?" I mean, he was so cool.

CW: But there was a time when the jazz musicians were playing to those two thousand folks, and they were rocking while the jazz musicians were playing.

WM: That was another brief period.

CW: A brief period, okay.

WM: That was a brief period when that was happening. It was a little golden age. You can't expect a golden age to go on forever.

CW: That's true.

WM: But you have to be willing to exert the effort required to maintain something of value, or else you won't maintain it. First you have to identify that it's of value.

It's like when we used to sit up in those ignorant movies in the seventies. I went to see every one, man. Oh, boy! The latest pimp would come out, and, you know, just the profanity and the ignorance. We loved it! Even now, as a grown man, the legacy of that ignorance still resonates in me. You couldn't find anything too ignorant for me to like. You remember how it'd be like a good hip, funk soundtrack, man. The whole theater'd be grooving. You know, just the title track'd come on.

And then the next generation of people became people who were well educated but who gravitated toward that type of image. Ignorance became an aesthetic, like a statement. Now you have Duke Ellington replaced by—what we would be doing. I mean some of this stuff we'd be doing on gigs. I joined this band when I was twelve. You never question it. Man, it's so much fun. You know, you're out there. You're having a good time. Then you start to say, Well, man, you know. . . . You start to see it a certain way, the ignorance of it. It's a hell of a lot of fun. But it's like anything in your personal life. You know if nobody maintains it, it's not going to maintain itself.

CW: What are the major obstacles for the maintaining of this tradition that you're talking about? I know you've been more evangelical in the deeper sense of that term than most when it comes to jazz education, exposing people across race and region and nation to jazz. But what are the major obstacles? Is it the market? Is it moneymaking? Is it interest you're talking about? Is it just the fact that we live in such a thin-lipped and thin-blooded culture, such a hollow civilization? So that most folk are trying to hook up with some sentimental mode in order to be addicted to get through the mess that they find themselves in? Because there's a sense in which what you're talking about is jazz signifying this mature wrestling with what it means to be human, and most Americans of any color are not interested in that. They muddle through, rather than confront the challenges.

WM: You know I don't agree with that.

CW: Tell me how you disagree.

WM: I think that people, they're just like me and you. We all are dealing with the same thing. When we know about something, and we know that it's hip, that's what we want. If we don't know it's hip, we don't know. And I don't think the people really want garbage.

Now, jazz musicians, we've made a lot of mistakes, too. First, we're reacting to the whole twentieth-century trend in art to separate itself from the opinion of the populace so that you're not hurt. Because you're always getting hurt. People don't understand your music, they don't like it. So what you do then is either you say, Well, okay, this is not designed for them to like. Or, I don't really care if you like this or not. This is what I'm hearing. Well, then a certain humanity is not going to really be in your music if you're not subjecting yourself to that criticism, to the hurt of that. So we started doing things like you catch a solo all night, and we used the same form with every tune. People are not ever going to like that. You've got to be Charlie Parker to pull that off, and we're not going to get too many more of him. So that style is not going to sustain five hundred musicians. You go to a club now, you know a cat sits down and plays one song, it'll be twenty-five minutes, man. You're not going to win that battle. You are not going to win that battle because the tune that you're trying to fight with is not the right one. So there are certain things that we have done as musicians in reaction to the initial rejection of our music.

But then on the other hand, we have the whole decline in all of American musical culture. It's just a general whole decline, really, just filtered through a teenage sexuality. And we remember being teenagers. That's fine. Hey, man, I loved being in that funk band. I'd be lying if I said I didn't. It was fun.

CW: What'd you like about it?

WM: Well, the main thing would be the women. [*Laughter.*]

CW: That's teenage sexuality.

WM: The truth of it is what it is. You go play a jazz gig, you know. . . . You can have a stimulating conversation or something, but that's it. You wouldn't say, "Well, okay, where's the funk gig?" because you want to have a social interaction that's going to be meaningful. [*Laughter.*] And what has happened is once you release kids from the whole thought of being adult, once you have adults who want to be kids, well. . . .

I talk to students all the time. They say, "Our music." I have to say, "Son, you don't have any music. There are people sixty years old putting out these things and determining what you're going to like. You didn't make that. There ain't no teenagers doing this. You're all not determined enough, and you're a victim of it." But it feels good to be a victim of it. So you're fighting a losing battle. You're talking about words; and they're talking about, gee, well, you know, I've got puberty on my mind, and I'm going to deal with it. So it's a very complex situation.

CW: You really do believe, though, that—in this sense I think you're a real democrat with a small *d*—you really believe that jazz can become as popular as hip-hop and rap music?

WM: No, I don't think that.

CW: No?

WM: I think it could one day. But now, in this climate? No. You don't have that type of shift in the public consciousness yet. But it will come. And I'll tell you why it's going to come.

CW: By means of what? Education? Appreciation?

WM: What's going to happen with the popular culture. It is on its way, believe me. It will become so self-indulgent, it will celebrate ignorance, it will have such a lack of soul, and it will reflect such a disdain for the taste of the public, that eventually people are going to just say, Wait a second. Not this. And then we will collectively say, We want something else.

And you just have more and more of these things. You know, you have two rap musicians recently killed. People making all this money and they want to kill each other and curse each other out. And the media laps it up and elevates it. The younger people lap it up. That becomes black behavior. That's real. Man, I'm being real. I say, "Wait a second, man. If somebody's saving your life, and they take you to the hospital, and the doctors there were trying to take all these bullets out of you, were they real, too? Or were they fake?" We've got to a place where the definition of what something is is absurd.

CW: Do you think that can be turned around, too?

WM: It will be.

CW: The most despairing aspects of American society today, and black culture in particular, would be the plights and predicaments of so many young people.

How do we recapture a sense of joy, black joy? I grew up in the black church. We had a sense of joy, and that was qualitatively different than pleasure, you see. Because in the same way that the sense of awe before the sheer majesty of the universe, as well as the horrors and terrors of life, transfigures fear, that joy is a way of transfiguring a certain kind of—how would you put it? A certain kind of horror that can be shifted. When you come into a situation in which you know you're down and out, that's already a sign that you're wrestling. You just don't have enough strength. And joy is a way of empowering you back into that struggle. Whereas pleasure is something else, you see. Pleasure is something else. It's not simply that it's more tied to individuals as opposed to groups. But it doesn't have the spiritual depth that joy does. We've got a lot of black pleasure around here, a lot of black

pleasure. And sometimes of high quality. But we don't have
enough black joy, you see. Tears of joy. When was the last time
you saw black people crying *tears* of joy? Not tears of sorrow. You
don't cry tears of pleasure. The point is, what institutions and in-
frastructures can we revitalize for the black joy to flower and
flourish? And the treasures are still in place. Some civic associa-
tions are still in place. There's still some black joy out there.
There's black joy in families. Not as much as there ought to be,
not as much as there ought to be.

WM: Yeah, I think it will be turned around.

CW: How will that take place, though?

WM: I don't know how. Because it's going to take the consciousness of
a lot more people than just me. You know the only way one person
could figure it out is if he were a dictator. Now, if we had a dictator, he could turn it around. Believe me, it would be turned
around in a week. Like Singapore. You know, you go to Singapore? Boy, you wouldn't have that problem there. But in democracy things take a lot longer.

CW: The emergency is in place now. What is the ground of your hope?

WM: Human history.

CW: Human history's not too good a. . . .

WM: Let me tell you. I'm going to tell you. You and I sitting up here,
talking in the Schomburg Center. We've got trumpets up here.
You're still wearing your Afro. You know what I'm saying? You've
got books out. You're respected as an intellectual. Now, 150 years
ago, man, you would be down there talking about, "Damn, it sure
is hot out here." [*Laughter.*]

CW: That is some evidence. Now whether that's enough evidence is
another question.

WM: It's enough for me.

CW: But are there any conditions under which you think your hope could be snuffed out?

WM: None!

CW: None whatsoever?

WM: As long as I'm alive. That's just in me as a person.

CW: Is it because of the freedom that you know as a human being and as an artist that reveals that no matter what the situation is, there's always some possibility it could be better?

WM: Yes. Plus I believe in God.

CW: But what does God mean to you, though, Brother?

WM: It's just ascendent consciousness. This is something that I learned from my great-uncle, from my grandmother, from my father. The world was messed up for my father. He had to deal with not working and a bunch of kids. Arguing and fighting, he and my mother, dealing with their relationship. Being completely disappointed. He thought he was going to be some great musician. He ended up teaching part-time in schools, not making much money, shuffling two and three jobs. Unhappy. You know, years of that. I could feel deep disappointment in him, deep, profound. He never complained to me about it. He wasn't a drag. He was totally cool, but he was overwhelmed by what happened to him. I know it. I could see it.

CW: Right.

WM: But he had this thing, this belief in this thing. Now, I don't know what that was. He had this belief in that thing. And that thing— All these musicians, Sonny Stitt—I can remember meeting all those musicians when I was a boy, and they have that, even when they're beat down. You know, maybe a cat'll be an alcoholic, maybe he'll be a drug addict. They still have that thing in them, this belief in this as a belief. And it's a thing that cannot be broken or taken out of you.

CW: It cannot be extinguished at all.

WM: It can't. It doesn't make any difference. That's right. I'll go to any type of school. I'll go to any area. I know that the problem is not having enough time. I know you could start with five of your partners and clean up any block in Harlem, any fifty. That's what I know. I don't wonder about it. You and I and four other people, we could start today, and every day work two hours a day. And in five years, boy, they'd be saying, Damn! Look at what they did. But the question is, Who wants to do it? You know what I'm saying? Who wants to do it? It's not, Can it be done?

You know, people have struggled much harder than even the most struggling people out here now. The world is a hard place. Somebody said, "Yeah, it's easy for you now. You working." I wasn't working like this all the time. You know I felt all the whole disappointment of all the people in my family: my great-uncle, my great-aunt, my grandmother, my mother. I could feel all that. And it was profound, and it was real. Not just them; all the people in our neighborhood. We didn't live, you know, "let's get around the piano and play some blues tonight."

We're people, man; we're trying to figure out what's happening. You don't know what somebody else is dealing with. And when you think the negative, it brings that negative out in that other person. But when you think, Yeah, all right, baby. Come on in here. You know? What's happening, man? Sit down. What's that? You play trumpet? Yeah, put your horn up. You sound sad, but you all right. [*Laughter.*]

CW: And it can sound better if you practice.

WM: Yeah. That's where the jazz musicians would be coming from to me. You know, soul.

CW: I think that's why for me Coltrane is *the* towering figure. I think not only because of his technical mastery of the craft but also because of a deep and profound spirituality. He understood that compassion means having a commitment to something bigger than he himself.

WM: That's right.

CW: And it was inextinguishable.

WM: That's it. That's what it is.

CW: And for him it was God consciousness, too, very similar to what you're talking about.

WM: Yes, it was everybody.

CW: It was all embracing, it was global, it was cosmopolitan. But rooted in Hamlet, High Point, North Carolina, and Philadelphia, you see. That's genius. And that legacy is still very much at work, I think, in your life and in your own work.

WM: Yes, sir. Yes.

CW: But one wonders about the next generation, although I guess they said that about us, too.

WM: You know, I don't wonder about them because I'm out there dealing with them.

CW: And you see great potential?

WM: They're doing a lot that's dumb. But they're being told stuff that's dumb. These kids, there's nothing wrong with them. Now, I guarantee that there can't be too many people who don't work for the Board of Education who have been in more schools than I have.

CW: That's for sure.

WM: Sometimes two or three visits to a school a day, all over the country. And the black schools really are the same. The education system is very segregated. But all our kids are suffering. Don't think that it's just black kids. There's a lot of stuff that's put out here to make people think separately. But we're not separate in this country. We are together. And this is something that I discovered.

CW: Mmmm hmmm. You can see how we're so interdependent.

WM: And the fact that we in this country refuse to address that with the type of earnestness and the energy that's required to really deal with it—

CW: That's the problem, though, you see.

WM: Hey, we've all got to deal. Sometimes you've got to be the one that accepts the pain of it. If you go on a bandstand, and you're the only one who can really play, you can't say, "Man, you're all sad." Because you can't play without them. You've got to say, "Well, damn, I guess I might have to wait five years to play with you all, when you hear the records I want you all to go get."

CW: Mmmm hmmm. You've got to work with others.

WM: You know, we lose sight of that because we are in pain. So what? You're in pain. People have been in much greater pain, you know. The pain is in the world. It's out here; it's going to get you, no matter who you are. In this country, you know, we're dealing with imagery a lot of times, and the imagery overpowers the reality. We've got to deal with the reality

CW: See, that's why I would go so far as to claim that when we really look at jazz and the blues, we're really talking about a certain existential way of being in the world, which is a level of maturity that is rare in this barbaric century. And we're not just talking about America; we're talking about Nazism, Stalinism, European colonialism, patriarchy, homophobia, all those forms of evil that attempt to dehumanize and infantilize people, keep them children, keep them in Peter Pan land, you see. I see you as a kind of jazz ambassador, whether you're blowing your horn or whether you're dispensing your wisdom.

WM: You don't have child prodigies in jazz. You've got people who can play good when they're eighteen or nineteen and twenty, but you don't see a seven-year-old kid get up and sound like Pops. You're never going to see that.

You will not see that because this music deals with the world a certain way and with humanity, and it requires a certain type of adult understanding of the complexities of things that are going on. So you talk about Duke Ellington, you're talking about your genius, the most sophisticated, most adult.

CW: But in some ways, though, I would think that it still is about Louis Armstrong and Duke Ellington because jazz is fundamentally about a mutual respect, a learning how to relate to others in such a way that you *listen* and learn about good manners. Not in the cheap sense of bourgeois civility. But in the deeper sense of how you're going to relate to the other so that you can be a better person and that other can be a better person. Now, that's jazz, too.

WM: Yes, sir.

CW: As a way of life, with a disposition toward reality as a mode of being in the world, you see. And Duke Ellington is not just a matter of his artistic genius, and it's not just a matter of his elegance. But it's his way of being in the world. There's something that's profoundly soothing about his presence, even on the screen. Be-

cause he's somebody who in time and space has enough confidence to have to deal with tears, lament, struggle. But he's
smooth in dealing with it, even though you know he still catches
some hell.

WM: It's about relationships and how you negotiate yourself through.
Like you and I. Right now I'm talking all the time. We're talking
about music. I'm here to talk. But given the dynamics even behind your saying "Mmmm hmmm," I'm trying to determine
whether I should shut up or not. [*Laughter.*] You know what I
mean?

CW: Always working back and forth.

WM: Like he said, "Mmmm hmmm." Now he could be saying,
"Mmmm." That means "shut up." [*Laughter.*] Jazz music is our
art form that was created to codify democratic experience and
give us a model for it. Jazz music was invented to let us know how
to listen to each other, how to negotiate. Because when you're
playing on a bandstand, you might hate what somebody else is
playing, but you've got to play along.

CW: Mmmm hmmm. You've got to play.

WM: And you've got to listen to people. Because if you aren't listening
to them, you can't play with them. And you're forced to play with
them because you're on the bandstand with them. Not only that,
they're making up what they're playing. So in addition to them
imposing what they think on you, they're making it up, too. So it
has a whole logic. It's going along the way that they want it to go
along. And you can't turn around and say, Play what I want you to
play! And then if you listen, you might find that we've got a new
song with that. Yeah. . . . And they might be listening to you,

thinking, man, why is he playing that thing? But that's what our music is about: negotiation.

And that's how our music is, and children don't have that type of judgment. Whenever I go around to a school in America—high school, college; it doesn't make a difference—I always tell the kids to play a song. And I listen to that song that they play. I listen to it very carefully, and I let them play the whole song. And when they get finished with the song, I look at the whole band, and I say, "Now, tell me what she played, the first person who soloed. Anybody in this band, tell me what that first person played." No one ever, ever—this is out of hundreds of schools—ever knows what that person played. So you don't know what she played? Did you listen to what she was playing? No, you know, I didn't— Why didn't you listen to what she played? Well, you're playing jazz. She's soloing. You're supposed to be accompanying. You're the rhythm section. Why were you not listening to what she was playing? I just wasn't listening.

The same thing is true of the jazz bandstand. The drummers and the guitar players always play too loud. They have the loudest instruments. Those with the most make sure that those that don't have nothing don't get nothing. I say to the drummer, "Why you playing so loud? Do you realize that no one can hear anyone else in the band except for you? Why are you doing that?" "You know, I'm just used to doing it." He's not doing it on purpose. He's used to doing it. You know that people solo all night? Me, too. I know it. I'm telling you. I'll stand up and do it and ask myself in the middle of it, Why am I still playing? And the rhythm section will just be playing and playing and playing, and you'll just be playing.

It's a lack of compassion and understanding of the bandstand. And no interest in listening and actually interacting with other people. And just a disrespect for the process. It's like what we have for America: a disrespect for the process of democracy. People say, "Why should I go vote? They're going to do what they want anyway." That's a disrespect for the process. Why should I play soft? Everybody's going to play loud anyway. Why should I play short? Everybody's going to play long. Why should I listen? They're just playing the same old stuff. So it's a disrespect for the process, and we have to try to help that out.

CW: You don't have a common language without mutual respect. You don't have mutual respect without wanting to spend time with people. And you don't want to spend time with people unless you really believe in the people. And one of the points that was, I think, most salient for me in so many ways, or especially most poignant, was this tremendous investment of self of Brother Wynton in young people believing that they can in fact become interested in the music or more interested. Never giving up. You can't create a common language unless you fundamentally believe that people will be interested in it and respect them enough to give them time enough to come around to it. And that takes patience.

But patience is a sign of maturity. Just like when you're talking about parents raising kids. You know? That's patience. If you don't have patience with a child, you're not going to be a good parent. That's just the bottom line. That's the truth in life. But it has to be mutual respect. We do need to respect one another, and I think that that cuts both ways. I think that the younger generation needs to respect the older generations, and that we older generations need to respect the younger generation, that we all have something to give. You can't create a common language without assuming that everybody has something to give that is of worth and is of value. It doesn't mean that it's going to be equal. Because if you've been around longer, and you can relate more wisdom, then people need to listen a little bit more. That's just a fact, you see. Toni Morrison's giving a lecture on how to write a short story, and I'm giving a lecture on how to write a short story, you don't need to listen to me that much. That's just a fact of life.

WM: For me, all my learning is from jazz music. Music is a collective wisdom. And you can hear that in the sound. A sound is a powerful thing, man. A sound is not a joke. A sound is a mystical thing. And a lot of times what our young people do, the sounds that they are hearing are so—they're sounds of such profound ignorance and bad intentions.

Sometimes I listen to this music, and I just thank the Lord for letting me know what it is. I remember when I first heard "Train." I was thirteen, twelve. We all used to go to these house parties. We used to wear leisure suits then. I had a peach leisure suit with a brown-flowered shirt on. I still remember it. So I went to this girl Shawn Jones's house, which is in the country. And I came home from the party. And it didn't go like I wanted it to go. It was not memorable.

I said, Man, I'm going to put on one of these records. I put on this record of "Train." Oooohhh. And I started listening to that record every day. John Coltrane, *Giant Steps*. I put that on. I said, Damn, John Coltrane, we bad. My daddy had these records, you know. So I'd bring it to my boys across the street. We'd be listening to Stevie Wonder or something. I'd say, "I want you all to check out this Coltrane record, 'My Favorite Things.'" I put

"Train" on, and they'd be like. . . . [*Laughter.*] So I said, Well, damn, I guess it ain't everybody can like this. But then, two or three years later, my boy began, "We were up in there listening to Coltrane." See, so this music, it's going to be around. There are going to be people who are going to play it. It might be some people from Australia, man. Thirty years from now, forty, fifty years. People might have stopped playing jazz in the United States of America. There'll be a kid somewhere, and after she finishes hearing those records, she'll say, "Man, I could play like Monk." Boom! There you go.

That's how art works, you know. It's on a stream. That's what the Martians are going to ask for when they come here. People will be sitting around with all their cameras and stuff, and they're going to want to know something about science. And the Martians are going to say, "Yeah, but we want to know where we can hear some blues." [*Laughter. Applause.*]

Patricia Williams

13 December 1996, City University of New York

CORNEL WEST: Do you view the law in all its complexity as a source of hope specifically for people of color?

PATRICIA WILLIAMS: I see the law as an instrument, and it's very hard for me to answer that question in any sort of monolithic sense. For me, hope is a force that ties people together in an almost theological sense. And law is an institutionalized version of what ties us together, and it negotiates between the individual and society and the state. And in that sense I suppose it ought to be related to the concept of hope. But the law itself is neutral.

CW: It's something applied. But can it function as a weapon, as an instrument, in sustaining hope among a subaltern people?

PW: Yes. It certainly has been that. The civil rights movement is a marvelous example.

CW: That's interesting.

PW: And you can certainly think of many other instances in which the actual interpretation of particular laws in courts at every level was infused by a sense of hope, was fed by an appeal to hope. Hope written into law.

CW: Right. That's what I was going to say. But what about the limits of the law as a weapon. I think of the fetishizing of law, the ascribing of magic powers to the legal system. Of Thurgood Marshall in the early fifties thinking that after *Brown v. Board of Education* we'd actually have integrated schools within five or six years because the law said so. How do we actually specify and delineate some of the limits of the law as a weapon?

PW: Yes. It's interesting that one of the great tools of the civil rights movement was civil disobedience, which goes to lawlessness.

CW: That's right. That's right.

PW: Which by its very contrast pushed the law to broaden its boundaries.

CW: The younger generation has had a much more brutal relation to the repressive apparatus of the state, even after the civil rights movement—with the levels of incarceration, with the levels of police brutality, all in the name of cleaning up the streets, like Guiliani here in New York since he's come into office. How do you negotiate these kinds of tensions, both within the legal academy as a legal theorist and literary artist and then also as someone who is deeply concerned with the everyday realities of working people and poor people? I would think that it would be very difficult to make a case that the law can be emancipatory, given the brutal face of it that they're exposed to.

PW: In criminal law I'm very, very concerned about the employment of state force. You know, every time somebody is put in jail, there's an argument about the limits of state force. And that is at least to some extent a political one, and it's a legal one. And lawyers have a role in that. The question of what's law and what's legitimate is a declared one, in that sense. It's a sort of dictatorial one. Law is always that. Hopefully it's informed by democratic impulses that are more than the tyranny of the majority but are tempered by some sort of balance of interests.

I'm very concerned that we have imported notions that we formerly considered illegitimate and made them legitimate and
therefore law. It doesn't make it any more morally right to me.
And I think that part of my job as a lawyer is to point out the tension between some of what we call law and some of what is defin-
itively declared as illegitimate in international human rights con-
ventions.

CW: What would be an example of that?

PW: Well, certainly some aspects of our prison conditions. The kinds
of police practices that, unfortunate as they are, are being revealed in Philadelphia and New Orleans and in certain precincts
in Milwaukee. You can be as cynical as you like about the police
and black communities. However, it's blacks who are most conservative and want the police there. Blacks really want good police protection.

CW: They're 90-some percent of the victims of criminal behavior and
need protection.

PW: But these may indeed be the same people in the same bodies who
are most distrustful of the police.

CW: That's right.

PW: So in that sense there is simultaneously an appeal to law as well
as a disaffection for law that needs to be reconciled.

But I want to stay on this question of having faith in the law.
In order to understand my concern about what's happening with
the law, about what's formerly illegitimate now being written in
as a legitimate exercise of state power, I think we need to look at
the patterns of rhetoric and the patterns of the way we talk. Look
at things like capital punishment. There's an example recently
of a man in Washington State who begged the authorities to be

hanged because that's how he wanted to be executed. "Step it up. Hang me." And the debate, the public debate, as well as the legal debate, as well as the debate among ethicists, sidestepped the question of the legitimate limits of state force and focused on his choice. "Well, he chose to, who are we to stand in his way?" It was sort of like the discourse about the economic, rational actor. I think it sidestepped the question of judges' responsibility, society's responsibility, limits on state force. It turned out that this man had actually strangled all his victims, who were children, and gotten an erotic pleasure out of strangulation.

CW: Right. So he *wanted* to die that way.

PW: Yes, he wanted to die that way. And some people say that that's just his choice. But it seems to me that this is the point at which we as a culture become implicated in torture or erotic fantasies of whatever. And we come to that absurd result by an ideological capitulation to almost an econometric model of humanity. Public execution becomes rewritten as publicly assisted suicide rather than privately assisted suicide. It seems to me that when we rewrite the scenario of criminality, of arrest patterns, of imprisonment, and of execution in those terms, then we can step back and not take collective responsibility. We say, "But they just chose it," which is, I think, a dangerous state of mind: "That has nothing to do with us." "That has nothing to do with me."

I would make a similar point about Tawana Brawley or even Susan Smith. The focus on Tawana Brawley lying or not lying ended the story for many in the public. You know, if she lied, then we can throw her away. We can throw the body away. We can throw out the fact that she was found in some state of mutilation—whether it was self-mutilation or somebody else did it to her, possibly her mother or her father. Nobody questions how she got to that state. Nobody really puts at issue the fact that Tawana Brawley was a minor, that her story, to say nothing of her name, should never have been in the public eye. Child protective services should have stepped in and taken care of that young woman long before she arrived at the age of sixteen. But she was still a minor when all that happened. And she was put, it seems to me, in an untenable position. People never asked questions about, for example, her abusive stepfather. She had been beaten up by him even in a police station. She'd repeatedly run away.

Susan Smith. Again, we only ask, "Did she lie or not? If she lied, give her the death penalty." Yet Susan Smith also alleged that she was a victim of child abuse. We don't make those sorts of connections. And so for me the application of the law has to be tied up with these longer, larger questions of our history, of our culture, of who we are in some cultural sense. On the one hand there's still a civil sense that somebody is too young to drive or too young to drink or too young to vote. But the victims of gross abuse, the victims of tremendous neglect at far younger ages, still can be held criminally responsible to the extent that they're now talking about the death penalty. That we can really treat these young people as trash and throw them out without any sense of connection to these institutional failures all the way along the line seems to perpetuate those institutional failures.

In some ways it leaves me ending up wanting to appeal more to some of the institutions we have. I don't want to be understood as saying that because I believe in the cultural analysis of the law, therefore I'm appealing to lawlessness. I think that I'm making a much broader appeal to a whole series of connected steps that are rooted in law, that are rooted in politics, that are rooted in culture, and that we have allowed to fall into disuse.

I think cultural assumptions are employed very contradictorily. They're good in some instances but not in others. We feel much more sympathetic to the victim of domestic violence when it is Nicole Brown Simpson, who fills a certain imagistic stereotype.

I have lots of problems with that imagistic stereotype of somebody who is very sexualized in the public eye, who's made extremely vulnerable, who's almost made the quintessential pornographic slasher victim. But if in fact she had actually run away from O. J. Simpson that first time he hit her, she would be somebody with six months of waitress experience with two children, going out on her own. If she rejected any aspect of his support, his apartment, whatever he set her up with, she'd be on welfare. Like her sister was. We don't talk about Denise Brown's having been on welfare. That is not present in the public mind. Nicole Brown Simpson's sister was on welfare for a while when she fell on hard times.

It seems to me that we have not connected the sense of ultimate victimhood that Nicole Brown Simpson represents with the kind of victimhood that many women who are on welfare represent because we have figured the woman on welfare as a black woman. You know, Clarence Thomas's despicable sister. It doesn't occur to us that the same fragility with which we imbue Nicole Brown Simpson might be extended to the woman on welfare who has been the victim of abuse and might also account for some of the resentment, by black women on juries, against Nicole Brown Simpson—which some have said is really class resentment, although I think it's actually much more complicated.

Of course, this is not a competition. This is not to say that black women or white women are ultimately any better treated as we both lie on the slabs. But it's coded very differently. Black women get victimized by figuring them as those who can never be raped because they're so tough and they're so old, even when they're minors. And they're such liars, even when they're minors. And white women are those who must repeatedly and endlessly be raped—because they're so inherently ravishable.

CW: It says a lot about the sexual politics as well as the cultural politics.

But I want to turn to this issue of a sense of history, this stress on subtle narrative. Storytelling in the most sophisticated sense. Do you think that this sense of history, the use of subtle narrative, can in fact become more widespread in the legal academy, such that it would allow the academy to speak more clearly and more powerfully to the kinds of issues that you've just mentioned?

PW: The law is the history of subtle narratives. The idea that somehow critical race theorists introduced storytelling into the legal academy is ridiculous, absolutely ridiculous. I was a trial lawyer. We were taught how to construct a story, be persuasive, present a narrative. This is all about how to tell a story. I don't do anything different.

CW: But the legal positivists and others claim to be highly suspicious of subtle narratives.

PW: Certainly what I have done is speak in the first person, and I think many people have taken that to be much more indicative of the personal—as though it's autobiography, as opposed to a rhetorical argument. In fact some people have taken the most absurd things as autobiographical. As if I actually see rabbits or ghosts or polar bears, rather than use them as literary devices.

And certainly, you know, I have only very rarely used the first person in a courtroom. I might introduce it in my writing, in a parabolic sense. I use a lot of parables. I don't present myself as emblematic of all black people. That is something I've tried not to do. When I write an autobiography, people will know it. But what I'm describing is not so much autobiographical as it is an attempt to negotiate the sense I have of a self with a sense of groupness imposed on me.

You know, I walked into a shoe store, I asked to try on a pair of shoes, and the salesman brought me one shoe. I said, "I'd really like to try on both shoes." And he said, "Well, when you pay for both, you can have both."

CW: This is in New York?

PW: This is in New York. And it was jarring. It's so extreme in some sense. He looked at me and said, "Well, what if there were hundreds of you in the store? I couldn't—" But there weren't hundreds of me. In fact I was the only customer in the store. There were a couple of other salespeople lounging around doing nothing. And some of my writings are about myself as of hundreds of me. Which is a different enterprise. It's writing about myself as I walk through the world with this fragile, social, and perceived-to-be-suspect profile surrounding me. It's focused to a certain end. In some ways it is I who am on trial. I set myself up on trial in some ways, making a case about the black experience. And I hope not an essentialized individual me, but really as a way of bringing out the absurdities of the essentialized social shell in which we as blacks operate.

CW: One of the ways of hiding and concealing race is to tell lies. Which is another form of storytelling. And yet that's not viewed as storytelling per se. When you think of all the lies that have been told about indigenous peoples, black people, and so forth, it takes a lot of energy to sustain those lies. But those are stories. Particular kinds of stories that are false, refutable, and unwarranted. And yet when persons come back with counterstories, it's they who are seen as storytellers, and storytelling is devalued. It's a kind of double bind. I'm thinking specifically of the legal academy and the ways in which it has historically dealt with race.

PW: Yes. Well, here's a story. I was listening to the radio, and somebody was reading a police report. A police report is a story, but we don't call it a story, you know. It's an "objective account." And this was the police account of a guy who walks into a bank somewhere in Queens. He robs it, and he's running down the street with a sack of loot. And a van drives up, some guys step out, and they mug him, stealing the loot. So he runs down to the police station, and he says, "Help! help! I've been robbed!"

Now this is a story. They were actually broadcasting it on the radio because it sounded so stupid. Right? A burglar with no brains. In a sense, it is a story because you could label that story "A Burglar with No Brains."

But if I then introduce the fact that the first robber was white and he was out to rob his local neighborhood bank but that the guys who came up and robbed him the second time were black, it becomes a different story. You realize that the second set of robbers' transgression seemed so much greater to this guy just because of their race. It's sort of a cultural parable, it seems to me, in which even though it was virtually the same crime, to the first burglar there was a trespass that went far beyond the mere act of robbery. In that sense it becomes a much more complicated story—but this is the point at which the law would accuse me of storytelling because I'm racializing it.

Yet it seems to me that race is an important ingredient of telling how the law responds. In the example I just gave, the "race-neutral" version of the story sounds foolish. It sounds stupid. It's the race story that reveals how race rationalizes an apparently irrational situation. And it seems to me that we have to take that into account. If we keep race as a secret narrative, then racial politics becomes simply stupid, or it becomes paranoid, or it becomes this thing that we don't take into account. But if you actually reveal the racial component, then we can get down to talking intelligently about what was really being valued here, and we can see that it's more insidious. It may make us feel more helpless. But it at least identifies what's going on in some way so that we do more than simply laugh about it. It may be troubling, you know. Maybe we still want to make a decision that the law can have nothing to say about this. But at least it is acknowledged.

CW: This is fascinating.

PW: I do think that race rationalizes irrationality over and over and over again in that way. It does so whether we talk about it or not. And if we don't talk about it, we make it more powerful.

CW: I was wondering what one says to the cynic who suggests that if we actually had a robust, uninhibited discussion of race, it would be deployed by the right wing, to help them organize and mobilize. Remember, for every member of the Democratic Socialists of America, which is the largest left-wing group in America, you've got seven members of the Klu Klux Klan. And so if in fact the Left wants to make race a major issue, it cannot but backfire.

PW: That argument assumes that the Klu Klux Klan has been lying there dormant until black people brought up the subject!

CW: Yes, yes. But you would admit that there are certain truths there in terms of the depths of racist sensibilities in the populace, though?

PW: Oh, I do think there's a tremendous depth of racist sensibility in the country, that right now we're in a historical moment in which fundamentalists of all sorts are coming out all over the world. But to me that is all the more compelling a reason to talk about race— and fast. You know, even in as relatively safe an environment as teaching, it's easier in some ways not to talk about race. But if I avoid the subject, all it does, it seems to me, is shift the burden of racial discord to me internally. I actually wrote *The Alchemy of Race and Rights* based on years of having taught in a particular environment and not talking about it. In fact, a lot of it was stuff I'd actually taken out of my computer and put in what I call my garbage can. There came some point at which I decided to integrate it into the ongoing conversation I was having with students. And I put those memos together, and that became *The Alchemy of Race and Rights*. But it does seem to me that the not talking about it goes somewhere. And part of what contributes, I think, to the high level of stress and mental illness among many people in black communities is not talking about it, is the fact that that becomes our little secret garbage pile. We sit on that garbage, and it doesn't get filtered so that we can deal with it.

Again, I'm somebody who is very loath to prescribe broad solutions. But one of my greatest concerns is how law can be used to redistribute at least enough resources for things like education and employment. Those are just the starting points. It seems to me that those are two of our most important issues: how you can survive; how you can get enough to eat. So for me the issues of education, welfare, and employment are central. I believe that we need to refocus our attention onto the very young in our society, the very hungry, and those without.

CW: If we had a full-employment law on the books, do you think that it would be enforced and implemented?

PW: I'm not sure that it would be.

CW: Because on one level we've actually got laws that look beautiful. But you've got these weak mechanisms of implementation and execution that have to do with power, pressure, contestation, and so forth. I mean, we have antitrust laws, yet all these monopolies and oligopolies flower and flourish.

PW: I believe that the law can describe our better selves in such a way that we come closer to living up to them than if they are not written into the law. That's why I don't underestimate the impact of law to shape our expectations and to shape our ability to insist on what is right. It is better, for example, that we appeal to child protective services in a case of suspected child abuse than not.

And so many on the Right have pointed to the fact that suddenly instead of working, blacks are swelling the welfare rolls, that these people have given up the moral call that was the true meaning of the civil rights movement and have gone on welfare instead. What actually happened was that suddenly, because of the challenge of civil rights, many states could no longer deny welfare benefits to the poorest in society. And people who had all along been entitled to welfare went on welfare.

But the impact of the new welfare laws falls on young boys, on boy children, as well as girl children. It is dramatic, drastic, and tragic. I would like to see some evaluation of what's going on in the great public rush to send mothers back to work with infants at home with no provision or funds for day care. Where are those children?

So even though we talk about welfare as a women's problem, it affects children who will be the next generation, one way or the other. I think that the fact that we arrest so many men is certainly of great concern. But I also think that women's depression and women's self-destructiveness are problems. Women are more likely to commit suicide than men, who are more likely to direct rage outward. But it does seem to me that women are in no less trouble, even though we don't have jails for suicidal and depressive actions.

CW: That's a good point.

PW: Another problem, in my view, is many Americans' sense of an unbounded right to the employment of private force. I'm particularly concerned about gun control. You can't have conversations about what's right and what's legal if you've got private militias saying that if you say the following, they're going to shoot you. Gun control and the drug trade are two of my biggest concerns. I think that they affect our ability to do anything else because they corrupt every other sort of democratic enterprise.

But what is of no less concern to me is the perception that some force of law, which should have integrity without question, has been implicated in the enormous infusion of drugs. I think that that perception costs us a sense of trust in our institutions. And that is a crisis, it seems to me.

That sense is precisely the larger cost of what happens when an entire precinct in New York is actually engaged in a conspiracy to peddle drugs and to shake down drug dealers. So people can be *guilty* and the victims of police abuse, or they can be *innocent* and the victims of police abuse. And when it doesn't seem to make a difference anymore, this creates a crisis in the faith that holds us together as a society.

And I think that racial divisions keep us from a coherent conversation about the extent to which this is really a question of the accountability of state forces across the board. Instead, blacks become a community hunkered down against government or distrustful of institutions when in fact *all* Americans have reason to distrust government. We need to see and begin to talk about how race divides us even on issues where we may actually share common ground. I don't think that the police abuse just black communities. It's much more focused in black communities, but lack of accountability is a pervasive social problem. The distrust of the CIA, you know, hasn't had so much impact perhaps in the black community. It's global—a question of whether you can trust what the army says about poisons or Agent Orange or napalm.

CW: Are there any conditions you could imagine under which you could see yourself losing hope?

PW: I think I would have to lose my faith that the continued effort itself is worth something, even if I don't see any positive result in my lifetime. And I don't foresee myself losing that. I became a Quaker when I was thirteen, and I went to meetings through much of my adult life. My considerable lapses probably indicate some ideological tension. But I do believe that if you work to change the lives or the minds or the conditions of one person a year, or three or four people, if you have that sort of impact on the life of another, you should consider yourself tremendously lucky. Because progress can be long term as well as short term.

I have to accept as a limit, for example, that Rupert Murdoch seems to own everything and that Rupert Murdoch is never going to agree with me. The press, the free press, is what keeps us informed. And the free press is no longer free but really a for-profit organization based on entertainment and commercials. Or it is held by three people who aren't going to print all sides of an issue. There is nothing I can do about that.

But I can say that I'm really glad that we're in the age of computers. This is going to be a very powerful medium, one capable of subversion. But that is a site that is still very much in its infant form. And because it's so much in the process of being developed, it's still capable of a lot of artistic forms.

One of my most hopeful examples of that is some guy who lives in the projects in Champaign or south of Chicago somewhere. He went out, and he bought a radio receiver from Radio Shack for about $300. He put it together, and it broadcast for exactly one mile, roughly the circumference of the housing project in which he lives. And he broadcast revolutionary radio all day, every day. People from the projects would come in, and they'd broadcast. From what I'm told, the FCC spent something like $800,000 trying to shut this guy down. He'd hear them coming up the stairs, and he'd toss the one-watt receiver over the fire escape and keep on broadcasting. [*Laughter.*]

But apart from that kind of drama, there's so much that is being invented in the way of new informational technology, where so few can reach so many—even without the permission of the great media barons, in the traditional sense. As for the price for access to it, certainly the technology is still out of the range of most people—*most* people, period. But it does seem to me that as the technology becomes more and more available, again, we will be dealing with more and more inventive young minds in inner cities.

I do think that the price of computers will plummet. We're still at an early stage of this technology. I think it's a little bit like the telephone, but it's much, much more comprehensive in terms of its potential impact. And I think just in terms of the impact that computers and emerging forms of technology are going to have on our sense of privacy, the sense of copyright, this is just going to be transformed. I think that it will very much revolutionize how we communicate among ourselves. And I foresee a creativity as well as just a subversiveness in the process itself that will ultimately make certain aspects of the control of the printed word quite outdated. Though I do think that there is a possibility that it will come out exactly the opposite way. That we'll end up with Big Brother.

CW: It might backfire on us, too?

PW: It might backfire. But I also think that the battles that are being fought now could anticipate a different kind of undoing of the power now being wielded by those who control the media.

As a lawyer, to me it's important to argue cases about access to media, access to control of media. Affirmative action in this as well as other spheres. I mentioned education and employment. But it seems to me that the media has been a very, very important part of what I've argued about in terms of providing legal access, legal mandates.

There was an article in *Time* to the same effect, some time ago, reporting that Microsoft went into a public library, and they were going to install computers as part of an experiment in the Bronx. And the salesman was apparently extremely snide to the librarian, saying, "Is this going to be like *The Gods Must Be Crazy*? Is this going to be like the Coke bottle dropping on their heads?" And the librarian apparently said, "No, I prefer to think about it like a field of dreams. If you build it, they will come." And come they have. I don't know if you've seen it, but hundreds of people are lining up to use it. Just from far and wide they're coming out to use it.

CW: Wow!

PW: And the end of this story was that there's this guy in Brooklyn who's on the Net as often as he can get on. And you know what he's doing? He's downloading the instructions for building a computer. And he's building it slowly at home. He said, "Yep. Next time I'll have another little board," and he's putting it all together. So there's some interesting hopefulness there.

Haki Madhubuti

25 October 1996, Chicago

CORNEL WEST: Next year Third World Press will celebrate its thirtieth anniversary. You made the institution, edifice, infrastructure, and reputation all around the country and the world. It's really quite a tribute to both you and your particular role within this larger tradition of black self-determination, of institution building.

HAKI MADHUBUTI: Thank you. Yes, we've been publishing what we consider African-centered literature for the last twenty-nine-point-some years. And I've been privileged to be a part of this since its beginning.

CW: But more than a part. You've been actually the leader, the founder, the initiator, and the sustainer in many ways. But I know it's a team effort.

HM: Yes, it's always a team effort. And I think that the only reason that I am able to do much of the work is because we do have these teams. We have these men and women who have been working very hard, and often they don't get as much credit as they should. I founded the press when I was twenty-five years old—with Johari Amini Hudson and Carolyn Rogers. We were all students at the time. And I lived in a basement apartment about the size of this table that I shared with other animals. [*Laughter.*] I didn't even know what they were. And I had published one book, *Think Black*, in 1966.

And so I called Carolyn and Johari together and said, "Let's start a publishing company." I had earned about $400 from a reading. I said, "Let's use this money to start our publishing company." So that's how we started out. In the early days we were all young people who believed that we could do anything we wanted to. And we were not going to take no for an answer. And really it's very, very important. We started out in my basement apartment, but we moved to a storefront right over here on Seventy-eighth and Ellis. Just right across the street from where our school is now. Then right next door we opened up the Institute of Positive Education in 1969 in the other storefront. Specifically to deal with the whole question of ideas in education in terms of young people.

CW: You've always been so unique because on the one hand you're an artist and poet with a very sophisticated sensibility and artistic creativity. And on the other hand an institution builder, kind of a businessman as well, trying to make sure that you keep a foothold in the industry, and bringing in young people to keep the institution going. How do you carry out both those roles at the same time?

HM: Well, I'm a product of the black arts movement, of the civil rights movement, of the sixties. And I grew up in a very impoverished community. Never having enough food, never having enough—I mean I lived in a house where the lights would be off one day and on the next day. You understand, it was very difficult. My mother basically ended up being consumed by the system. Became an addict, an alcoholic. And OD'd at the age of thirty-five.

Some things impacted me very early. That's all. So I've been on my own since I was sixteen. I left Detroit and came to Chicago and lived at the Y. Finished high school. Tried to get a job. Couldn't find any employment. But what gave me consciousness was finding black literature at thirteen, fourteen years old. See, my mother asked me to go to check out *Black Boy* by Richard Wright, and I refused. Because I didn't want to go to the white library and ask for anything black because I was full of self-hatred then. But she said, "Son, go get the book." And so I went to the library, found the book on the shelf, put it to my chest, walked to the unpeopled section of the library, and began to read. And as I read, it felt like I was just getting slapped in the face. I had never in my life been hit with ideas of such hope and insight. And of course I saw a lot of myself in *Black Boy.* So I checked the book out and went home and stayed up all night reading. The next day I was not necessarily a different boy, but I began to see the world differently.

When I got here to Chicago and got out of high school, I couldn't find a job. And I joined a magazine-selling group. I was at my wit's end because I couldn't find a job anyplace. I've graduated high school, I'm six foot one, 131 pounds, like a walking skeleton. There was this brother and his woman. They had two cars. They had this makeshift office somewhere down on the South Side of Chicago. I went down there. And they were recruiting all these young black people to drive across Illinois into Missouri, stopping in small towns selling magazines, *Jet, Ebony, Life*—this is 1960.

And the spiel was you'd lie about your trying to work your way through college. Now the interesting thing about this was that no one had ever talked to me about going to college or university. Never. It was not in my mind. So in June, going across, stopping in Galesburg, Illinois, I knocked on this door. A man came out. I went through my spiel. I said, "Sir, I'm trying to work my way through Howard, and I have debt," and everything, and boom boom boom. And he smiled. And I guess I looked so down, he said, "Why don't you come in and have a seat?" And his wife was there. This was a retired man. And he said, "What are you majoring in at Howard?" And, you know, I lied about something. This man had graduated from Howard.

CW: Ohhhhh. . . .

HM: So he realized right away I was lying. And he said, "Son, just relax. Just relax." He said, "I know you would not be out here doing this if you did not need the money. I want to take a subscription to *Jet, Ebony, Life,* and one more. I'm going to pay you right now for them, give you the money. And I want to talk to you for a minute." He said, "Obviously you've given me a line to sell the magazines. I understand, and I can appreciate it. But you need to try to go to university or some college." Now, that's the first time anybody— this is a perfect stranger—sat me down, and he gave me $20. And he said, "Just take it easy, and don't worry."

Later we got into East St. Louis, and I got very sick from eating this bad chicken. And the people I was with left me at the hotel. They're gone. I'm by myself. I've got $2.50. Everything I own I've got with me. I've got my cornet with me. I've got my slide rule. I've got my one suit that I had from my mother's funeral. My one overcoat, underwear, and a few other things. Everything I've got I'm carrying with me.

CW: Everything you own right there.

HM: So I pulled myself together. I did day work. Now, day work for men is different than women at that time cleaning white folks' homes. Day work for brothers, you go to the docks, you see, where there's a train dock at this point. You go, and you stand in line for a job. And you just load trains. Okay? So I did that. I used to spend my evenings in the library. For about two or three weeks I did that. And I said, I've got to find something more stable. And I joined the military. I joined the army.

Now, the interesting thing about this is that there's three of us, three brothers, and the rest white men. The white men for the most part have been drafted. We joined. So I'm reading Paul Robeson's *Here I Stand* on the way to basic training, which is at Fort Leonard Wood, Missouri, in 1960. Get off the bus. I've got Paul Robeson's book in my hand with this big black magnificent face on the cover. The drill sergeant sees this. He snatches the book from my hand. He said, "What's your Negro mind doing reading this black Communist?" Then he says, "All you women up against the barracks." There are not any women there. The whole indoctrination's starting now. They break you down and build you back up. So we jumped up. And I say, "Just let me have my book." He holds my book over his head and commenced to tear the pages out. And gave a page to each of the recruits and told them to use it for toilet paper. So now I am questioning my own sanity. You know, why did I join this military?

But I was also reading John Oliver Killens's *And Then We Heard the Thunder*, which was about a black man in World War II. And what John told me and taught me was that when you're outnumbered, shut up, stand back, plan. And I decided three things that morning, that early morning, in Fort Leonard Wood,

Missouri. One, that I am African, I am black, and I would never, ever apologize for being black African again.

The second thing was that I had to know about my culture. So I put myself on a reeducation program. Now by that time, I had gone through Du Bois, I had gone through E. Franklin Frazier, I had been introduced to Garvey. I was aware of Carter G. Woodson. But after this happened, it became very clear that I needed to study with a mission. And the mission was to become a self-informed person of African ancestry.

And the third thing was this: that if it was indeed the ideas in Paul Robeson's book that scared this man so much that he would destroy it, then ideas were very powerful. We all tap-dance to somebody's ideas, in a sense. So the question for me was, Whose ideas am I going to tap-dance to? Am I going to tap-dance to my own ideas or somebody else's?

CW: Given this very, very poignant, powerful journey of your early life, what was it that kept you going? Your situation, I think, was much more difficult than most black people's, let alone white people's. What were the real grounds of hope then?

HM: Well, when you read this literature, you find out that we are, I think, a people of surprising hope. You see that over and over again. But also what happened is prior to my being released from the military, I would come to Chicago. I was stationed at the missile barracks at Arlington Heights. And I would come into Chicago and volunteer at the DuSable Museum of African American History for Margaret Burrows and Charlie Burrows. At that time the museum was still in their home: 3806 South Michigan Avenue. I would come in every week and volunteer. And I became like an assistant curator, you know. I was only about, what? Nineteen, twenty years old. But the point is that they had one of the best libraries in existence at that time. And I would just devour their library. Now, Charlie Burrows had an interesting background because he was raised in Russia, the Soviet Union. And both spoke Russian fluently. And he introduced me to the work of Tolstoy, to Dostoyevsky, and then the political writers, too. I mean Lenin, Marx, and all that.

CW: You were reading those Russian writers early on. Now, was it something about the Russian writers, from Tolstoy to Chekhov and others, that spoke to your own sense of being in the world?

HM: Well, their sense of dealing with the peasantry. You know, dealing with poor people. Fighting the powers that be. And of course with Margaret and Charlie Burrows both being very Left in terms of politics, I got it all.

But I always give credit to Charlie Burrows and Margaret Burrows. They built this museum from nothing. And I was part of it in the early days. I saw it from when it was in their home, the first floor and the basement, to where it is now—one of the largest African American museums in the country. So I got that institution building from Margaret Burrows. And I think the important thing about it is, to do it with nothing. An interesting thing about Margaret Burrows is that she always had this self-reliance.

CW: Yeah. Using her own resources.

HM: Right. Charlie Burrows was the same way. Plus it gave me the other idea. Margaret encouraged me to put the poems together. In 1966, I published my own book, *Think Black*. I took it to a printer on the West Side of Chicago, had it published in, you know, about thirty pages.

CW: Distributed it yourself?

HM: Yeah. I sold it on corners. I stood on Seventy-third and Cottage Grove, and we were in the midst of the civil rights movement, the black empowerment movement. I was working with SNCC and CORE in this city. And I was selling at the rallies and everything. But Dudley Randall had also started Broadside Press up in Detroit.

CW: Detroit. Exactly.

HM: And I asked Dudley if he would consider publishing my next book, which is *Black Pride*. He published it and wrote the introduction for it. So at that point he became my publisher. And I took what money I had and started Third World Press here in Chicago.

CW: Wow! This is rich. But I want to get back to this question of grounds of hope. Because you'd begun by talking about the tradition itself, of surprising hope. Here you have a couple, a progressive black couple, in a deeply conservative, if not reactionary, country, who are creating this institution. You're interacting with it, inspired by their example. And then you're off to founding your own institution.

HM: Yes. But even prior to that. I've gone through that period Dudley Randall comes into my life. Dudley Randall's one of the premier poets in the country. Started Broadside Press in 1965, '66, in Detroit, Michigan. Dudley Randall was really the first black man I met from the middle class, you see. So Dudley and his wife had built their home from the ground up. This is in Detroit. Now I was astounded. I've lived in apartments and all that stuff all my life, and here's a man who built his house from plans. And then after about twenty years or so, he decided—maybe it was a bit longer than that, about thirty years—he said, I'm going to start a publishing company in my house. And that's how Broadside Press got started. So he was a great influence. So here I had two institution builders right in my life at a very critical time for me.

Then Hoyt Fuller came into my life. And Hoyt Fuller was the first black man I had met who had traveled around the world. So he had immense knowledge. He had basically taken over the editorship of *Negro Digest*. When John Johnson started *Negro Digest*, it was like *Reader's Digest*. Hoyt Fuller took it and completely reoriented it toward creative writing, toward new writing, not pulling anything from other stuff. So Hoyt and I began to interact. And it was very positive because Hoyt saw something in me—I was very intense, a very intense young man—so he began to ask me to do reviews for *Negro Digest*.

Now, I did not mention Malcolm X because I never even met Malcolm. But Malcolm gave me my voice, especially coming up through the early sixties. Malcolm was on fire.

CW: On fire.

HM: And so Malcolm gave me this sense that you can really do this if you want to. So we've got Malcolm X. We've got Margaret Burrows and Charlie Burrows. We've got Dudley Randall. We've got Hoyt Fuller. And then here comes Gwendolyn Brooks.

CW: Here comes Gwendolyn.

HM: Gwen was teaching a creative writing course to the Blackstone Rangers here in Chicago. Right down in Woodlawn. So Hoyt and I and some other writers said, "Let's go down and visit Miss Brooks and see what she's doing." So we jumped in there. And I was starting a very serious relationship. It was tenuous and difficult at first because, you know, I'm black, black.

CW: Right.

HM: And Gwen is used to European writers, you know, and she didn't know anything about the major black political thinkers. She knew the literary writers. So we began to introduce her to Garvey and so on.

CW: So you all helped politicize Gwen. And yet she was already a master.

HM: Yeah, she was already a master. No doubt about it. She was one of the best poets writing in the country at that time, as today. But being naive, and being young, and being arrogant—and that's what youth often brings—she had to really settle us down. We had arguments and stuff like that.

CW: At that time would you say that she was a follower of Martin Luther King, Jr., concerned about black suffrage that early on?

HM: Yes. Very much so.

CW: But at the same time more kind of an integrationist. Or had she already shifted?

HM: Well, surprisingly enough, only integrationist to the point of personal relationships. Gwen has always lived in the black community. Never been in awe, as far as I know, of white folks. While the Negro writers who are basically trying to lead black publishing are doing anything they can to get with the white publishers, she made a political decision in '68—'67, '68—to go with Broadside Press.

Now, obviously there are a lot of other things happening at the same time. I'm involved in the black arts movement. I'm traveling a lot more. In 1968, I got invited to a workshop at Fisk University. Did real well down there. Got two job offers. Got a job offer from Talladega College and one from Cornell.

CW: Well, you'd already published.

HM: Yeah, I published two books. And that was why, really. Now, see, what I learned at Cornell was this: I'd watch these white writers. And I'd say, How can they live and write? What was the secret? What were these writers living on? Their university salaries. So I thought, How can I deal in on this? [*Laughter.*] So when I got offered these jobs, I said, I'm going to go in and try to deal with this. And so they invited me to Talladega to speak. And of course once I finished speaking, they said no. No way in the world.

CW: Too radical.

HM: You're not coming down to Talladega. Not today. In fact, we may not even pay you. So I took the Cornell job, Cornell University. I was the first black writer-in-residence at Cornell. This is during the same year as the takeover.

CW: The same year as the takeover!

HM: Yes, some of the students doing the takeover were my students. I was there for that. Then while I was at Cornell, *Ebony* did this long piece on me. And *Don't Cry, Scream* came out that same year.

CW: That thing took off.

HM: *Don't Cry, Scream* sold close to half a million copies. It jumped. It jumped. It really helped all of us.

Now, okay. So there's this core called *hope*. And like I say, my basic philosophy is to be a realistic optimist. And I learned something else, which is that I believe in kindness. I learned that from Gwendolyn Brooks.

CW: She says her religion is kindness.

HM: And being around those persons, primarily Gwen, poets, Margaret, gave me a lot. I didn't have to ask for it. They gave it to me, and they didn't expect anything in return other than: Do your best. Do your best.

CW: Be yourself, and do your best.

HM: Do good. And as a result of that, I had this very deep foundation. Obviously, you found it in the literature. But when you have mentors, like Hoyt Fuller, and Gwendolyn Brooks, and Margaret Burroughs, and Charlie Burroughs, and Dudley Randall, and later—when I taught at Howard—Sterling Brown and Andrew Billingsley.

But the key point of a lot of this is that I never wanted people to say that I started these institutions for myself. All right? So that's why having a job and working in academia was so critical. Because it's the only kind of job you could have where you don't have to answer to somebody who doesn't even like you for eight or nine hours a day. And you had maneuverability. So especially when *Don't Cry, Scream* hit, I began to speak all over the world. People would just call me: Come speak to my group. So I would come, and the money would just go back into keeping this stuff going, keeping the stuff going.

CW: So how are you sustaining yourself emotionally at this time? I would think that with that kind of intense schedule, you were lucky you didn't have a breakdown. You're flying to these things, you're still writing, you're speaking, you're institution building and politically active. How are you working all this out in terms of your life?

HM: Well, obviously the people that you surround yourself with are very important. I met my wife back in 1969, '70. She was a young woman who came out of the projects on the West Side and decided that she was going to make something out of herself. And so she ended up going to the University of Illinois, coming out around nineteen, twenty years old. Went to the University of

Chicago, got a master's degree. Came out at twenty-one years old. She did her master's work on my poetry and other poetry of the black arts movement. And we were all young people, and our energy fed off each other.

I had also begun to read some of the Eastern writers. I began to practice yoga and meditation. Wherever I traveled, I would try to visit the spiritual institutions of the place, especially if I was traveling outside the country. Trying to get some insight. I changed my diet, became a vegetarian, and really got talked about quite a bit—they called me the "wheat man," you know. Now it's nothing.

CW: There were not too many black folk who were not eating meat in 1971. [*Laughter.*]

HM: So all this was happening. And at the same time, it was always good to come back home because we were grounded in this institution building. And there was a certain amount of peace here. When we came back home, it was like we were doing something. Even though we only published one book every six months or one book every seven months, it was something. We were doing something that we could measure.

CW: Yes. Very important point, very important point. And bringing in new people all the time, mainly young people.

HM: Young people—only young people. In fact, my wife was teaching at a local college, Kennedy-King College here in Chicago. And once we decided to go full-time with our school in this little storefront over there, we needed teachers. And she said, "Okay, I'm going to leave tenure track." You know, solid position, twenty-one years old, master's degree from the University of Chicago, you can't get any more solid than that. Her mama almost flipped. She thought that she had lost her mind. It was a major sacrifice. Because all we could pay her was $100 a week, $400 a month. No benefits, none. So with that kind of sacrifice, that kind of commitment, it just made you say, Okay, I've got to try harder myself.

And she was not the only one. Other people came and did the same thing. We had occupied an apartment building down here; we had about four or five of our families all living in four or five apartments down here, trying to build this thing. And the key point here is that this was our community. And that's what's missing today. Two things are missing today. One is community, whether it's in terms of family, extended family, or church. And the other thing that's missing is a movement. See, we all came out of the movement. And this movement nurtured us, this movement took care of us. We had surrogate mothers and fathers. We were all involved in a mass movement, we were involved in a struggle. We'd go places together just to be politically involved. And so whether it was through the Congress of African People, or CORE, or SNCC, we were involved. And then trying to build these institutions. Now, one of the reasons we really moved toward these institutions is because we felt that when you talk about people who are serious about their own development, it has to be institution based. And the only institution in the black community that had any kind of serious independence was the church.

And so all that stayed on in the back of my mind. I said, Now, this black religion has got something to it. And around that time I made my first trip to Africa, and I began to go regularly after that. And I was flirting with Islam. But when I got to North Africa, I knew that wasn't it. I said, I'm not going this way. And so I came back home.

CW: What was it that you saw that convinced you that you're not going.

HM: Well, the position of black folks.

CW: Oh, yeah. You're still subordinate.

HM: That's right. Very subordinate. If Malcolm saw something different, I didn't see it.

CW: But this takes us back to the issue of spirituality and hope because I've heard you mention Howard Thurman. He has had some impact on you. How early was it that you first encountered his works and the impact of them?

HM: I never met Howard Thurman. I encountered his works basically in my sojourns through bookstores. In the religious section, I said, What is this here? I had read, obviously, James Cone's *Black Theology and Black Power* and this other brother who did the first book on the black Muslims, C. Eric Lincoln. But Thurman was speaking more to the heart, you know, and not so much to the mind. At least that's how it hit me, that here was a man who was truly concerned about the person. I guess the soul would be the best way to put it. And so I began to read him regularly.

CW: But I would think that there would be very few young people of your generation coming out of the black freedom struggle, especially the young black nationalists crowd, reading Howard Thurman.

HM: I don't think anybody was reading Howard Thurman.

CW: Very much so. Because there's something very unique about Howard. You allowed Howard to speak to you even though very few, if any, of your generation did.

HM: Well, Howard Thurman spoke to me. You know I was part of Operation Breadbasket, and I was part of all the demonstrations, pretty much all the major demonstrations here in Chicago.

I learned an awful lot. What I learned was essentially this whole question of discipline. I've always had to write in the midst of struggle. And so this is why I always tell young people I'm blessed. And I don't back up over it at all. I'm blessed. I'm free. And the reason I'm free is not only because I realize that there is a greater power that's orchestrating this but because I realize that the orchestration is only at the minimal level. Most of it's left up to us. See what I'm saying?

I basically believe in all religions. I believe in all of them, and I don't believe in all of them. I believe in the religions whatever they may be, whether it's Christianity, whether it's Islam, whether it's Buddhism, whether it's Sikh, whether it's Hindu, whatever. Because I feel that each culture produces its own spiritual force and that they're all equal at that level. And who am I to say who's right or who's the greatest or who's superior and who's not?

In terms of my own body and my soul, there are four things I do: Do good work, one. Be kind, two. Three, avoid hypocrisy. And four, try to help as many people as I can while I'm alive. This is what living a spiritual life means to me. My wife says I should have been a minister. And my answer to her is that I'm not going to be hypocritical. I'm not going to lie.

CW: This is a kind of ministry, though. In a broad sense. Because it's service. Ministry is about service.

HM: Well, I guess you might say that in a broad sense, yes. I began to realize that the two significant institutions that our folks built from ground one without any help from other people—especially people who don't even like us—are, one, church and, two, schools. And so I chose to be involved with trying to build a school.

But all of this, Brother, at one point deals with again, goes back to, the fundamental problem of what's missing in the black community: community and that spirit of community. And the community can never be like the old community. We can never go back to that. But you've got church communities, you've got political communities, you've got cultural communities. All kinds of communities exist.

And that's why our school is so important. Because in essence it's a community. You see, our students will call my wife "Mama Sophicia." They will call me "Baba Haki." So we're their surrogate mothers and fathers while they're with us. And that carries on in terms of everything that they do.

We give them the same kind of quality education that they would receive at the best private schools. You know here in Chicago we've got the Lab School, the Latin School, and so forth. They're going to get the same kind of thing here, but they're going to get it in a cultural context, with a value system that was African centered. So when they leave our school, they're going to know who they are. They're not ashamed of themselves. They've got the self-confidence. They've got the skills, they know what they can do. And growing up sometimes all the classes will visit Third World Press because they'll see a black business over here. We've got black people building a business, which is one of the major African American publishing companies in the world. So they'll see that. They'll say, Well, okay, we can do that now. Now, when we were located on Cottage Grove, everything was in one building, so they saw it every day. But to walk into this place, you know, it's impressive.

CW: Yes, it's very impressive. Very, very impressive.

HM: And that's why we bought this place. See, we're down here. We're in two storefronts on Seventy-eighth and Ellis. And this Catholic school's right here in the middle of the block at Seventy-eighth and Ellis. And we said, "What about this school?" All the time we said, "What could we do if we ever had this school?" This is 1969, '70. We were saying, "What could we do if we had a place like that?"

CW: And twenty-one years later you own the school.

HM: We own it, right. But with a lot of pain, a lot of sacrifice.When the school came up for sale, quite naturally we wanted to bid. So the archdiocese goes to the real estate agent and says, "No, it's closed. The bidding is closed. You can't bid." I say, "Well, what do you mean we can't bid? We've been in the community for over twenty-some-odd years. Why can't we bid on this property?" So the white man says, "No, you can't. I'm sorry, but you can't bid on the property. It's closed."

So at that point I say, Who can I talk to? Who can I talk to so I can get at least our bid in? So I called some of my Catholic friends, and they said, "Haki, you need to talk to Bishop Gregory." He's the black bishop on the South Side. So I called Bishop Gregory. Never gets back to me. So I call again and leave the name Don L. Lee. See, I changed my name in 1974. I got a call back the same day from the secretary. And he said, "Bishop Gregory asked me to ask you, Are you the poet down there?" I said, "Yes. I really need to talk to Bishop Gregory about something very important. Do you think I can get just a little bit of his time?" So I went out there to the southern suburbs to meet with him.

And so I got out there, and the bishop was there. He had a big smile on his face. He said, "Yeah, I read your poetry in the sixties." I said, "Please, Bishop. . . ." And we began to talk. I told him that I almost became a Catholic. I was a very sharp student. I wasn't being challenged in the public school. But I couldn't afford to go to a Catholic school. And so I told Gregory all that. And I told him that he would not have to worry about selling us this property. We'd never deface it, we'd never dishonor the tradition that's there.

And when I left, he had written a letter to the cardinal and gave me a copy of the letter, which basically said: Not only should our man be on the list, he should be at the top of the list. So the next day the white realtor called me and said, "I don't know what you did, but I got a call from the cardinal's office to put you on the list."

CW: This is the same person who said you wouldn't be able to—?

HM: Yes, be on the list. And he said, "Yeah, but I don't know. . . . Well, now you're on the list. But the only way you can stay on the list is you've got to bring $50,000 in two weeks." So here is another challenge. I don't know how we'll get it. So I pulled together the board, and we talked and stayed up all night strategizing. And basically said, "No way in the world we can raise $50,000 in the next two weeks." So the only thing we can do is go into our own pockets. And that's what we did. We took from our pockets $50,000.

CW: But you all had enough money to—?

HM: Yes. See, at that point we had developed a board from a lot of people whose children had graduated from our school. Some of their children are among the leading advertising executives in the city.

CW: These are all black folks?

HM: They're all black folks, yeah. All black folks. And so we had at that time maybe fifteen, sixteen people on the board. And so we had to come up with what? About $2,000 or $3,000 dollars each.

CW: If everybody comes through.

HM: Yeah, everybody came through for the most part. And I put in a little bit more. I took what Sophicia and I had, we just took it all, about $10,000, and put it all into the school.

CW: Oh, God! You were the key to this, too.

HM: And so we got it. And then of course the next question was, How do you finance this place? Because they're talking about a million dollars here.

That was another whole battle, you know. So I'm saying that building institutions is a story. It's just a series of battles all the way until the time you can keep things going. But I think I never received any money from Third World Press or from the school. I was never on the payroll.

CW: You're not? No salary at all?

HM: No. I don't even take my royalties. Everything goes back into the press. So it has never been easy. Institution and family and writing and everything else.

I've always felt that we can do much more than we think we can do. Our capacity is much greater. It's much greater, much greater. What you always have to do is surround yourself with caring people, serious people. People who will put their resources on the line, you see, and help at the same time as you're putting your resources on the line. And never accept no. Just never accept no.

Never accept no. When you've got a vision or get an idea, then you've got to follow through, number one. But number two, realize that you're going to make mistakes. There are going to be failures, but that doesn't make you a failure. You understand? You just keep on struggling all the time.

CW: But I would think, there's a profound centeredness, a kind of spiritual strength that you have. Because I can imagine other people trying to do that, not being centered, and going under for a while. There has to be some real anchor that can hold you. Because those are some very fierce whirlwinds and storms that are going on there.

HM: Well, I believe in the spirit of goodness, you know. I believe that we have been made with the ability to be very good as well as to be evil. All right? And again, because of my children, and because we work with children. Working with children is so important. You just walk them to school every day, and you're going to be on your knees almost. Because of the innocence.

CW: It's in the smiles, the innocence.

HM: It's there. And my own children are doing so well. I have a boy—he turned nineteen on Wednesday, and we went up to have dinner with him. He's in the School of Engineering at Northwestern. And he's everything you could wish for. I say the same for all my kids. But to me that makes you stronger, you know.

I think of building these institutions and maintaining the family, extended family, as similar things. And again, it gets back to the church— Sometimes when I'm looking at this church I think in terms of how instrumental it was in the sixties. See, we were meeting in the churches in the sixties. But when the preachers got tired of us and said, "You all get out!" you're leaving, all right?

CW: Where are you going to go?

HM: Well, I said, Look, we're going to create our own institutions so nobody can tell us to get out. We've got our own things. We've got two auditoriums over here. We've got a dance theater meeting there now all the time. So we've got our own space. And that's what serious men and women do. You look at the development of any nation-state, you look at the power of the institutions. So if all we've had to look at is churches and maybe some of these Negro colleges and universities, we're in bad shape. So we've got to do what you're doing. We've got to have all of it. And the key point always is that what you do is not better than what I'm doing and that what I'm doing is not better than what you're doing. It's all needed. So if we're enlightened men and women, then we understand that.

CW: What's fascinating, one of the things that's always struck me, is how you always prefer, in a certain sense, not to be center stage. You're behind the scenes doing so much of the work, writing up the advance formulations and so on. But right at the time in which it's, oh, center stage, and of course most people are rushing for center stage whether they did any work or not, you've already laid this foundation. And always you have your say and so forth. But you've never really been obsessed. And this to me is rather rare among black leaders. And the Million-Man March is a good example of that in terms of your fundamental role in bringing people together behind the scenes so that the march could happen.

HM: Well, again, it's just that I don't feel that I'm a leader. I really don't. I feel that I am a point. And I've been blessed to be in the right place at the right time. This, my work, I think that's what I'm proud of. My work. I think I am a decent poet. I'm not the best poet, but I know I am a decent poet.

CW: You're far, far more than just a decent poet. But you're also a leader of a major institution, a set of institutions, in black America.

HM: Well, I just don't believe in tooting my own horn. I think that if it is indeed important, then it will live, and it will live beyond my generation. And then people like you and others will say that and continue to support it. I think that's the main thing. And I firmly believe that. My security comes in knowing that I've created something.

We did something. And I do think that one of the reasons I don't get beat up as much as I used to is because the people who don't even like me realize that this is important.

CW: You're trying to play an important role in the movement in such a very humble way. But at the same time it's also true that you speak your truths as you understand them. Which is to say, you take your stand. And anytime you take a stand, you're going to have folks coming at you.

HM: I think that I always try to be very positive.

CW: Constructive. Indeed, indeed. This is something. This is something.

Maya Angelou

19 February 1996, New York

CORNEL WEST: How do we talk about hope with all the suffering and the pain in the world today? What are the sources of hope?

MAYA ANGELOU: In the worst of times, incredibly, that's when hope appears, like a seed, like a bulb splitting. One never knows what it costs a bulb to split, a lily bulb or an onion, to split open. And that tendril to come out. But I do know that there's a song in Genesis, there's a statement that it had rained so long, that people had given up the idea that rain would cease. And then the Lord said that he would put a rainbow in the sky. There is that in Genesis. And in the nineteenth century, an African American wrote: "When it looked like the sun wasn't going to shine anymore, God put a rainbow in the clouds." Now that means that in the worst of times, in the dreariest of times, you can look right into the clouds and see hope.

CW: You know, Brother Martin used to say, "Only when it's dark enough can you see the stars."

MA: That's it. And yet the spring of hope is immersed in the winter of despair. You see a young boy, fourteen, fifteen years old, semi-literate. Maybe third generation on welfare. He doesn't know where he came from. He doesn't know he's already been paid for. But he walks down the street as if he has oil wells in his backyard.

[*Laughter.*] If I had come from Mars or Pluto, Uranus, I would look at the people on the planet, and I would say, "Who are these black Americans? Who are *they*? Who are they? How dare they hope with their history?" There is something that is so irresistible about the hope that we embody.

CW: You know, when I think of hope, I think of courage, and I think what has kept black people hoping, the best of our tradition is hoping, has been both a certain courage to be and a courage to tell the truth about America.

MA: That's right. We've got the courage to be on the one hand, and we've got the courage to tell the truth about America in relation not just to white supremacy but to other forms of evil.

CW: We've got a lot of male supremacy and homophobia and class arrogance and ignorance.

MA: Ignorance. It's all ignorance. It's the path, it would seem, of least resistance. This is ignorance: I know there's a homeless person over to my right, but I'm going to pretend he's not there. And I just keep walking. That's ignorance to pretend they don't exist, as if I am not like them. That's ignorance. Lack of courage, cowardliness. And courage is the most important of all the virtues. Because without courage, you cannot practice any other virtue consistently. You can't be consistently fair or kind or generous or loving. You see?

So when I look at where ignorance lives, it lives in my inability to admit that I am a human being. And that nothing human can be alien to me. And it's evil to remain ignorant. For the last few hundred years, there have been important and solid and honest doctors to attend the ill of racism, who have shown them, Here it is. Here it is, now. [*Laughter.*] In the late 1600s, there were some African slaves who wrote to their Dutch owners: How can you own me? I'm a human being. And how can you own my wife? How can you do this? And in 1996 there are still whites who say: Do you feel, do you think there's racism?

CW: That is evil, then.

MA: Yes, if you've been shown, time and time again, this is where the human spirit is assaulted. This is how the human spirit is bruised. And if my spirit is bruised, be sure that yours is bruised.

CW: The two go hand in hand. But this is partly a question of hatred and a question of fear. Bernard Shaw says it somewhere, I think it's in *Heartbreak House*, that hatred is the coward's revenge against those who intimidate them.

MA: That's good.

CW: On an individual and interpersonal level. Then when it's institutionalized—in slavery, Jim Crow, Jane Crow, segregation, discrimination on the job, attacks on black beauty and black moral character—then you've got a situation in which the struggle for hope requires deep organizing, mobilizing power, and pressure. Why? Because the only way you're able to fundamentally open your space is through some kind of collective struggle. So our individual spirits can sustain us in our collective struggle.

MA: I believe, Dr. West, that one other word for hope is *love*. Love. I don't mean mush. I don't mean sentimentality. I don't mean indulgence. I mean love. When I was seven, I was taken to St. Louis, to my mother's people. My grandmother was my father's mother. After I was there a few months, my mother's boyfriend raped me. I was afraid to tell the name of the rapist to my mother's family because the man said he would kill my brother. Well, my brother was then—and is now—my black kingdom come. He was older than I. But he was small. Even now he's five foot four and a half.

So he told me, "You know you have to tell me." I said, "If I tell you, he will kill you." He said, "I won't let him." I said, "Okay." So I told him. The man was put in jail, released in one day, and in three days he was found dead. It seemed he had been kicked to death. So I thought that my voice, my mouth, killed him. I stopped speaking for six years. My mother's family didn't know what to do with me. Fortunately, they sent me back to Stamps, Arkansas, to Mama.

Mama would braid my hair. I'd sit on the floor. She'd sit in the chair. She'd open her legs. I would sit way up close to her, both of us looking forward. I put my elbows around her knees. And Mama would pull that brush in my hair. And she would say, "Your Mama don't care what these people say about you, about you being an idiot or you being a moron because you can't talk. Mama know, when you and the good Lord get ready, you're going to be a preacher. Mama don't care what these people say, Sister. You just keep on reading that poetry. You just keep on being a good girl. You're going to be somebody, Sister." I used to think, That poor, ignorant woman. But here I am. That's love.

CW: Yes, that's love.

MA: Everybody else had given me up. Not only was I black and female and poor, but I was also raped, also a mute, in a little village in Arkansas. That was love, it was hope.

CW: Yeah, that's hope. That's hope! I love the way you interweave the hope and the love. Because, see, when I think about love, both in

my own life and in the lives of others, I think of that which keeps
one keeping on. Motion, movement, resilience, resistance.

MA: Yes.

CW: But the question becomes in contemporary black America today,
Is there a decline of such hope and love? And I ask the question
for this reason: that when we look at the black freedom struggle,
on the one hand we've got Garvey, and on the other hand we've
got King. Both obsessed with what? Love. Garvey obsessed with
self-love: black people had better learn to love themselves and
love themselves in such a way that they can keep moving against
adverse circumstances. King, love. Self-love predicated on not
putting others down.

MA: That's true.

CW: You can't love others until you love yourself. And loving yourself
is not a matter of putting yourself on a pedestal. It's a matter of
acknowledging your own humanity.

MA: There's a statement that was made in Latin: "I am a human being.
Nothing human can be alien to me." Now the statement was
made by Terence. And when you look in the encyclopedia beside
Terence with one *r*, in italics you see *Terentius Afer*. He was an
African, a slave, sold to a Roman senator, freed by that senator.
He became the most popular playwright in Rome, influencing
everybody as far as Molière. But in 154 B.C. this black man, not
born white or free or with any chance of ever achieving citizenship in the Rome of his day, said this incredible statement: "I am
a human being. Nothing human can be alien to me." That is so
incredible! If you can internalize the least portion of that, you
can never be the same.

I'm a black woman who has come through some things and who is going through something now. And if I live and the creek don't rise, I will go through something tomorrow. I could not have come this far without an understanding that there is no place that God is not. Whether I'm walking into the White House, or in South Africa in Soweto, or I'm sitting at a bar in Harlem, or in first class on TWA, there is no place that God is not. And years ago, James Baldwin and I used to have a song that we sang together. James Baldwin said, "The day after Alexander Graham Bell had a successful experiment in the telephone, some black genius sat down that night and wrote [*singing*]:

> I gotta telephone in my bosom. . . .
> I can call Him up anytime.
> Call Him up, I rang Him up,
> Tell Him what I want:
> King Jesus is on the line."

[*Applause.*] Okay. Everything. Thank you.

CW: Lord! That's just what I wanted to say. [*Laughter.*] Just what I wanted to say. And the reason why that black person sang that song is because, whether black folk want to admit it or not, given all the imperfections, it has been in the name of Jesus that the folk have been most able to preserve a sense of spiritual sanity and mental health. Now, I know that some say, Yeah, but that Jesus' portrait was like Michelangelo's uncle. They're right. But what the old folk also saw was that in the midst of their sadness and their sorrow and all the tears and agony and anguish and heartache and heartbreak, there was a love piercing through. And that love allowed them to love each other enough, to love their children enough, to say, Let me get on that telephone to try to make tomorrow better.

MA: I know that African American people have nursed nations of strangers, somehow saying, However you are, however backward you are in your humanness, I have the responsibility of treating you like a human being. I know I'm a child of God. This is what gives me the stuff to get up. Now, my work, the onerous task I have, is to remember and to be reminded always that the bigot, the brute, and the batterer are also—they are also—children of God. Whether they know it or not, it is up to me.

CW: When I hear that, I think of those black folk who have had the courage to be free under conditions of unfreedom. Because there's no way that the black freedom movement could ever have begun and sustained itself unless there were some New World Africans who said, "I am free and will speak my mind and will do what I have to do, even in a situation in which I'm defined as an unfree person."

For me, this has to do with being able to view yourself in the light of a story that's bigger than your life.

MA: Black people are still the last hired, still the first fired, still the butts of even white liberal jokes. Nothing has fundamentally changed. But the truth is that hope is always there. And there is that resilience, you see. And so a black man or a black woman, well planted in corporate America, knows very well. She may lie to herself. He may kid himself. But he knows. And if he doesn't know, he will be informed. Be sure of it. Oh, yes. And so the best thing to do, I would say this to the younger generation: Children, make yourselves some allies. This is imperative. Make allies. Wherever you are, make allies. First in your neighborhood, find yourself a black church. This is imperative. Go to the church wherever you live. If you live in an all-white neighborhood, go to a black church; introduce yourself. I'm telling you. Join the church that appeals to your intellect and your heart. Introduce yourself. Know some deacons, some deaconesses. Know some usher people. Know somebody. Because when the thing hits you—and be sure it will hit you—you need to pick up the phone and say, Elder Baker, this is Thomas. Let me tell you what's happening over here for me. And then the people will say, Oh no, we won't have that, honey. How many of us you want around there? I'm telling you, baby. And I live in Winston-Salem, North Carolina. I'm telling you. And I have the Reynolds Chair at Wake Forest University, and I'm on the board at Harvard, I'm on the board at the University of California, Berkeley. I have my foot right in the community. So that if somebody says to me, anything, I say, Elder Baker, let me tell you— [*Applause*.] The people will come. Never get so high and mighty.

CW: You've got to be able to say, Look, I am a small character in a larger narrative that goes all the way back.

So the question becomes, How do young folk situate themselves in a larger human struggle—love, hope, faith—and then have enough discipline, like Maya and Coltrane and a whole host of others, so that they're able to stand on track? Not just conviction, but part of a larger tradition that can sustain them, you see.

MA: Well, I would repeat that everybody here has already been paid for. And if you understand that in a part of your mind and spirit— whether the ancestors came from Ireland or Asia, Eastern Europe or South America, or from Africa, lying spoon fashion in the filthy hatches of slave ships—if you understand that somebody already paid for you, and that all you have to do is prepare your-self so that you can pay for someone else who is yet to come. And act on it, act with kindness and courtesy and generosity, develop patience so that your words don't just jump out of your mouth with rudeness and you cut somebody's heart away. Take a moment. That would be doing something, I think.

CW: Oh, yes.

MA: I think to realize that people stood on slave ship decks, and on auction blocks, and in cotton fields, down in terrible factories, without any chance of ever knowing what our names would be. What mad personalities we would foist on the world. They stayed alive so that we could be here and have the luxury of having a wonderful conversation. I mean, they've paid for this moment. Do you understand? So if we could understand that, we might be a little more gracious to each other. We might take some child, put our hands on some child. I know where we are today. I know that because of the rampant child abuse we are becoming reluctant to put our hands on children and young folk. But we have to take that back. We have to. Children want to be touched.

CW: Lovingly.

MA: Lovingly. But they need to be touched. From the moment the person leaves the womb, after having been there nine months in this gorgeous place, and suddenly there's cold air. What is that? And you've got to breathe that. Oh, God! Everybody wants to be touched. Every person wants to be touched. No one touches children anymore.

It still takes a whole village to raise a child. Nothing has really changed. We still need everybody. And somehow, yes. Our baton was dropped, yes. You see, a number of people made enough money, thanks to the struggle, they made enough money, they got enough jobs, so that they could move out of the community. And those who could move out did so, I'm sorry to say. And left a group of people who were not prepared. And then they, in their unpreparedness, because they were, again, economically assaulted, intellectually assaulted, spiritually assaulted, they then said, Who are these kids? And so people stopped raising the children and stopped putting their hands on the children. And something serious was lost. Something that we hadn't even lost in slavery was lost. And we have to claim it. We have to claim it with a kind of concentration and a kind of ferocity, usually only to be found in somebody about to be executed in the next half hour. We really have to dare. Dare! I'm sorry, but I must tell this story.

Last year the movie *Poetic Justice* was made. And I agreed— I hadn't seen all the script with some of the combinations of words. But they wanted to use my poetry. I said yes. And then John Singleton asked if I would come out and do a cameo. And I said yes, of course. I'd be delighted. I went out, and I was there for a week. The first day I passed a group of people, and there was a young man cursing. Cursing! Using combinations of words I'd never even heard before. But I passed, and I passed, and finally he and another fellow about his age began to curse, and they ran up to each other, and they were about to get into it. And the three or four hundred extras began to scatter because they were afraid of shooting. But one black man walked up to these two men, and when he walked up, I walked up. So he talked to one fellow, and I talked to the other. And I said, "May I speak to you?" He said, "———." I said, "Wait a minute. Let me say something to you."

He said, "It ———." I said, "Honey, let me talk to you, please.
Let me speak to you. Let me talk to you." And finally he calmed
down. I said, "Do you know you're the best we have? Do you
know we don't have anybody better than you? Do you know
everybody has paid for you, and they're all dead? Do you know
that? Do you know if you kill this young man or he kills you,
everything is lost?" I said, "Baby, let me talk to you."

The young man started to weep. So I turned him away from
the other folks, and I just walked down into a ravine with him.
And I talked to him, and I kept his back to the people. And I put
my hand on his head, and then across his face, kind of wiped away
the tears. The amazing thing is the man was Tupac Shakur. I
didn't know that. I didn't *know* that. But somebody has to put
their hands on somebody. [*Applause.*] Do you understand? So
somebody has to pick the baton up. And it is up to us. And if we
don't, we will disappear. [*Applause.*] That's the truth of it. That's
the truth of it. You have to take a chance that somebody may say,
Go to hell! Or worse. But you have to take a chance.

CW: Part of the problem, you see, is that you have to be secure in yourself to be able to affirm others.

MA: That's right.

CW: You have to love yourself enough to allow it to spill over and support others. And if you're having your own internal crisis with
loneliness and isolation, it's going to be difficult for that connection to be made, you see. And this is so crucial. I mean, when I
think of America, I'm reminded of this fundamental question:
What profit a man, a woman, who gains the world, but loses his
soul? Or *sells* her soul? We're all caught up in the world. But how
do you preserve any sense of the love and hope and faith and a

sense of integrity so that you can be useful in the struggle for
something bigger than you? See, the thing that always struck me
about the older folks was that even though they were living in
conditions in which to step out of place could mean you could end
up that strange fruit on the tree there, they were still able to keep
young black folk moving.

MA: Moving ahead.

CW: Exactly. And that was because they had some sense of service.
And a sense of sacrifice.

MA: And such a sense of sacrifice. I thank you for that. The word has
not come into my mind in too long. Thank you. *Sacrifice*, it's a
wonderful word. It's a wonderful condition. It's a giving, and it's
love, isn't it?

CW: Yes. But one of the interesting things to me is what happens to
love between men and women today. What are the conditions under which they're willing to be related and connected?

MA: All right. As you know, in West Africa, where most of our ancestors came from, there was, and is still today, matrilineal inheritance, and there was patrilineal control. So although I was mar-
ried in West Africa, and my husband might have had zillions of
dollars or pounds or whatever, my children would not inherit
from him. My children would inherit from my mother's people,
properly. So that all goods stayed in the mother's bloodline. The
father, however, has patrilineal control and still does in West Africa. He names the child. He says who he will marry, where he
goes to school, what land he will live on, and so forth. Slavery took
that possibility of patrilineal control away from us. But we had
matrilineal inheritance. And we still have it. And we have kept it
over centuries without knowing what we've had—we have had a

matrilineal inheritance. The mother and the daughters, the mother and the daughter and the daughter's children. So this is part of an Africanism, a social carryover.

Now, slavery so distorted it that we began to believe—black women began to believe—that we were it. The black men, after slavery, could not get jobs except as handymen and so forth. But black women could go into people's kitchens and work. So there was always this woman, this woman who kept getting bigger than life and stronger than life. Now, if you want to have a person controlled, Machiavelli wrote in 1507, then what you have to do is separate and rule, divide and conquer. So we have this already going, you see, this separation, which could be healthy if it was healthy. But it's a perfect ploy to use to further separate the people. So black women then began to feel, Look here. Wait just a minute. I pay the bills. But we need the men. So we put the men almost, almost make them—I'm sorry to use these hard terms and words—but we almost make them into pimps. You see? Because we don't demand something. [*Applause.*] The black man is capable of giving and wants to give, and that is to be a man. So he says, Look, you take this, and I'll see you next week. I get off next Thursday. I'll see you next Thursday. And unfortunately we put them into positions, and they then jump into the positions. Neither of us is guilty, neither of us is free of guilt. We are in it together. We will either survive together, healthily, or we won't survive at all.

CW: For me there are three crucial dimensions in terms of trying to understand the problems with relationships these days. One is economics. No doubt. When you're unemployed or underemployed, or when you have a high level of job insecurity and anxi-

ety, you're going to have trouble in your relationship. That was
yours. Oh, yeah. . . . [*Laughter.*] But I'll try and speak into that
thing. And that's real. The second is political. That when the
movement that focuses on your suffering is relatively weak and
feeble, you do feel debilitated, if not demoralized. And we're living in a moment now in which there is a kind of open season on
black folks. From three-piece suits, women black folk, to those
who are on the street with nowhere to lay their head. That rein-
forces the tension and the friction. Then we've got another dimension, which is personal. Which is we're living in a society that
is losing the art of intimacy. And by *intimacy* what I mean is the
courage to be vulnerable and to accent longevity in your relationship. We've got market moralities; we want disposable bodies.
And so it takes time to be able to really be vulnerable, to get to
know a person the way Adam knew Eve. That is to say, to know in
the sense of dealing with their insecurities and incongruities and
contradictions and tensions, and they get to know yours. Now,
one of the things about folks in the past, they weren't perfect, but
they knew they were in this thing together. They'll have to work
this out. That doesn't mean that you permit patriarchal subordi-
nation. But it does mean that it's not going to be meeting somebody on Monday and making the final decision on Friday. You've
got to work some things through. That's how intimacy is culti-
vated. And one of the problems, like this *Waiting to Exhale*, this
movie that's out now, it's really something. Because, I mean, it's a
wonderful movie because it's good for the world to know that
black women have a quest for romance; that's the version from
Hollywood. But we know that's been the case for a long time.
[*Laughter.*] Black women fall in love.

MA: Right.

CW: Can we get beyond the surface, beyond the cover of the book, and really learn what the depths of intimacy are all about? You can't sustain a high-quality relationship without those depths of intimacy. It's very interesting. I learned this in some ways from my wife, Elleni, from Ethiopia. Because I met her in October and told her I loved her at the end of November. And she looked at me and just laughed. [*Laughter.*] She said, "You don't love me. You don't know who I am." Yes, I do. Yes, I do. Yes, I do. [*Laughter and applause.*] She said, "No. In Ethiopia you don't even use that language for seven or eight months." And in so many ways it's hard for Americans, no matter what color, to understand that. Many do understand it, but it's hard, especially more and more for young people. Because they're dealing with the market culture in which intimacy is pushed to the side, and it's all about stimulation rather than nourishment. But the Million-Man March and a host of other events that generate some sense of possibility and motion, highlight this need for empowerment.

MA: The experience of the march was so overwhelming that I started to weep. And I'm not used to crying in public. But to look out and see all those black men, and I'm the daughter of a black man, and the mother of one, and the grandmother of a black man, and the auntie, and the beloved. I was overwhelmed by the beauty, the magnificence, and the incredible stick-to-itiveness. And the majesty of black men. [*Applause.*]

CW: Absolutely. Can I just add a footnote to that? Because I was with Maya as she was walking—you recall I grabbed you, and we just stuck together. Because the flow of tears was so linked to both the black pain and the sense of black humanity and decency in a moment in which black men are so maligned and vilified and dishonored and devalued. And to see that connection of such a towering artist on the one hand and the masses of black human-ity—predominantly, though not exclusively, black men—was a high that a crack addict has never experienced. It was a moral high. It was an existential high, you see.

MA: Now, whatever my dream, whatever my hope, whatever my aspi-ration and ambition, it is no greater than to be loved by my people. [*Applause.*] To be loved by *my* people first. First! And to hear those men. And as I walked with the Fruits of Islam and my own—my grandfather and my son—as I walked through, and the men, some young, old, plain, pretty, said, "We love you." This keeps me erect. What did it feel like? Sister, it was for you; it was for all the sisters. I was there for all of us. And every black man was there for all of us.

CW: Okay, just briefly, I want to talk about education; we're talking about an encouraging environment in which persons can be mo-tivated to take the life of the mind seriously, that's linked to a de-sirable future. Which means you have to have a community. Edu-cation is about community, family, teachers who care, and a sense that that education leads to something better: more exciting, more nourishing, more adventurous, a good job; it's a combina-tion of all those elements. And when you have motivational struc-tures breaking down, you usually don't have an encouraging envi-ronment. Or persons are convinced that the work that they are supposed to be doing will not lead to something better. And right now the larger crisis in the environment—which is partly eco-nomic and political and personal, as I said before—makes it dif-ficult for persons to be motivated enough to think that this kind of energy exerted would generate the kind of results that they want. And so we get a high dropout rate. We get demoralized teachers, those who are struggling against themselves, against the grain. And some who just say, Look, it looks more and more *hopeless*. Then we've got a job market, in part owing to the maldistribution of wealth, right? The 1 percent owning 48 percent of the wealth in the nation, they don't have a problem because they have an encouraging environment. [*Laughter.*] The top 10 percent own 86 percent of the wealth. The top 20 percent own 94 percent of the wealth. And you've got the 80 percent of the rest of the population struggling for 6 percent of the wealth. And sometimes they're convinced that their going through this educational system is not going to produce better jobs. Layoffs and so forth and so on. So we've got the economic and the political and the personal all linked together. And of course it's even more devastating in black and brown and red communities, owing to the history of white supremacy in the country. And so one of the things that I always accent for individuals is that they need to understand the whole but also have enough self-confidence and self-respect to persist no matter what because they still can make a difference. That's the thing. That's the thing.

MA: I mentioned those years when I was a mute in Arkansas and I read poetry. And I loved Shakespeare. I don't say I understood all that much, but I loved Shakespeare. I loved Edgar Allan Poe. I loved Poe so much I called him EAP. I loved Langston Hughes and Paul Lawrence Dunbar and James Weldon Johnson and Countee Cullen. I *loved* them. And then at one point in Arkansas— Black children in Winston-Salem, where I live today, still perform in church twice a year, at least twice a year. But when I was growing up, the children would perform during Christmas or Easter, and they had four little lines of doggerel. They said, "What you lookin' at me for? I didn't come here to stay. I just come here to tell you, This is uh . . . um . . . um. . . ." And somebody in the church would lean forward and say, "Christmas, honey." And the child would say, "Christmas Day," and get off the stage. And all the old folks would say, "Didn't he do nicely." Bless their hearts.

But during that period I would sit on the mourners' bench or in the children's pew, wherever Mama sat me, and I would think, if I could only speak. So at thirteen I decided to return to my voice. My voice hadn't left me. And I decided to use Portia's speech from *The Merchant of Venice* in Stamps, Arkansas. Okay? In the smallest church in town, and the whole town big as this stage. Because my grandmother was mother of the church and owned the only black store in town, and people were really often abused by Grandmother. They owed her money, and Mama didn't like that. So they would see me in the road, and they'd say, "It's a shame Sister Henderson's California granddaughter done gone mental." [*Laughter.*] Or, "It's a shame Sister Henderson's California granddaughter, you know. . . ." So I decided I was going to speak. I was going to use Portia's speech in *The Merchant of Venice*. I saw how I was going to do it. The announcer would say, "And now, little Mistress Maya will render her rendition—" I was going to say, "The quality of mercy is not strained. It droppeth as a gentle rain." And I was going to knock those people off the pews. My grandmother asked me, "Sister, what you going to render in your rendition?" I said, "I'm going to render a piece written by William Shakespeare." My grandmother said, "Sister. . . . You'll render Mr. Paul Lawrence Dunbar, James Weldon Johnson, Countee Cullen, Langston Hughes. Yes, ma'am, you will." So I did. But when I physically and psychologically left the condition that is Stamps, Arkansas, a condition I sadly warrant too many people right here in New York City dwell in today, I have found myself, I find myself now, and shall find myself as long as I'm alive and sentient, putting on Shakespeare whenever I like. I understand he wrote it for me. Four hundred years before, along the Avon, in London, wherever he was. He wrote it for me. To know what I felt like, he had to have known something—

> When in disgrace with fortune in men's eyes,
> I all alone bemoan my outcast fate
> And trouble a deaf heaven with my bootless cries.
> And look upon myself and curse my fate,
> Wishing me like the one more rich in hope.
> Featured like him, like him with friends possessed,
> I'm desiring that man's heart and that man's scope.
> And with what I most enjoy, contented least.

So here's the white man who wrote that in England; and I, a black girl on the dirt roads of Arkansas, used it for hope.

So I tell you that to say, Use it all. Use it all. Use Kierkegaard or Oe. Use it all. Make your students—let her, him—take García Lorca in his mouth, eat it. Eat it all. It is all for you. Don't let anybody narrow you down into some mean little tunnel [*sustained applause*] out of their ignorance. Don't! Don't do it! Don't do it. Don't do it. No. I refuse. I want to see the black students and the white students and the Spanish-speaking students, the

Native American and the Asian, the straight and the gay, I want you to take it all. All! All knowledge is spendable currency, depending on the market. Put it on in there. [*Applause.*] All of it. Yes! Yes, sir. Yes, sir. [*Applause.*]

CW: It comes back to that wonderful phrase: Nothing human is alien to me.

Catch the Fire

Sonia Sanchez

(Sometimes I Wonder:

> What to say to you now
> in the soft afternoon air as you
> hold us all in a single death?)

I say—

> Where is your fire?

I say—

> Where is your fire?
>
> You got to find it and pass it on
> You got to find it and pass it on
> from you to me from me to her from her
> to him from the son to the father from the
> brother to the sister from the daughter to
> the mother from the mother to the child.

Where is your fire? I say where is your fire?

Can't you smell it coming out of our past?

The fire of living . . . . Not dying

The fire of loving . . . . Not killing

The fire of Blackness . . . . . . Not gangster shadows.

Where is our beautiful fire that gave light

to the world?

The fire of pyramids;

The fire that burned through the holes of

slaveships and made us breathe;

The fire that made guts into chitterlings;

The fire that took rhythms and made jazz;

The fire of sit-ins and marches that made

us jump boundaries and barriers;

The fire that took street talk and sounds

and made righteous imhotep raps.

Where is your fire, the torch of life

full of Nzingha and Nat Turner and Garvey

and Du Bois and Fannie Lou Hamer and Martin

and Malcolm and Mandela.

Sister/Sistah. Brother/Brotha. Come/Come.

CATCH YOUR FIRE. . . . DON'T KILL
HOLD YOUR FIRE. . . DON'T KILL
LEARN YOUR FIRE . . DON'T KILL
BE THE FIRE. . . . . . DON'T KILL

Catch the fire and burn with eyes
that see our souls:

WALKING.

SINGING.

BUILDING.

LAUGHING.

LEARNING.

LOVING.

TEACHING.

BEING.

Hey. Brother/Brotha. Sister/Sistah.
Here is my hand.
Catch the fire . . . and live.

live.

livelivelivelive.

livelivelivelive.

live.

live.

Contributors

CORNEL WEST, perhaps the preeminent public intellectual of our time, is one of the most eloquent voices on race in America today. Philosopher, critic, and activist, he was described by the *New York Times* as "a cosmopolitan public intellectual among academic specialists. . . . He makes the life of the mind exciting." Professor of Afro-American studies and in the divinity school at Harvard University, he is author of the bestselling *Race Matters* and eleven other books, including *The Evasion of American Philosophy, Breaking Bread* (with bell hooks), and *The Future of the Race* (with Henry Louis Gates, Jr.).

KELVIN SHAWN SEALEY, a doctoral student and Dean K. Harrison Fellow in American history at the City University of New York Graduate Center, is a professor of communications at Hunter College and dean of students at the Packer Collegiate Institute. Mr. Sealey founded the Obsidian Society, Inc., and its sister company Obsidian, Inc., in 1995 in order to develop a model by which entrepreneurial initiative could be put toward improving the African American social and economic condition. *Restoring Hope* is his first edited text.

Poet, author, playwright, and actress MAYA ANGELOU needs no introduction. She was born in St. Louis in 1928. Her autobiography, *I Know Why the Caged Bird Sings*, spent 137 weeks on the *New York Times* bestseller list and has been translated into sixteen languages. In 1993, she wrote and delivered the inaugural poem for President Bill Clinton, and, in 1995, she delivered her poem "From a Black Woman to a Black Man," at the Million-Man March in Washington, D.C. Currently Reynolds Professor of American Studies at Wake Forest University in Winston-Salem, North Carolina, she is the recipient of numerous awards and honorary degrees.

Artist and humanitarian HARRY BELAFONTE has been called "the consummate entertainer." Born in Harlem but raised in Jamaica, he served in the U.S. armed forces, launched a career as a vocal artist at the Village Vanguard, and eventually became a recording artist with RCA Victor. His 1955 album *Calypso* became the first recording to sell over one million copies. A successful Hollywood movie star and producer, his films include *The World, The Flesh and the Devil, Odds against Tomorrow, The Angel Levine, Uptown Saturday Night,* and *Island in the Sun.* He also played a key role in the civil rights movement, mobilizing the international arts community in support of the movement. He is the recipient of numerous awards and honors, including the first Nelson Mandela Courage Award.

Senator BILL BRADLEY has been described as one of the most eloquent and prophetic speakers on the issue of race relations in our country. A member of the U.S. Senate since 1978, he is a former Rhodes scholar who went on to win an Olympic gold medal in basketball and to join the New York Knicks before entering politics. As a senator, he has championed critical legislation on education, health care, the environment, and gun control. He has also kept alive valuable dialogue on race, challenging every American to confront the reality of racial prejudice by asking each of us, "When was the last time you talked about race with someone of a different race? If the answer is never, you're part of the problem."

The Reverend Dr. JAMES A. FORBES, JR., is senior minister at the Riverside Church in New York and the first African American to serve in this position. Previously a professor at Union Theological Seminary, he has been recognized by *Newsweek* as one of the twelve "most effective preachers" in the English-speaking world and by *Ebony* as one of America's greatest black preachers. In addition to three advanced degrees, he holds ten honorary degrees.

HENRY LOUIS GATES, JR., W. E. B. Du Bois Professor of the Humanities at Harvard University and director of Harvard's W. E. B. Du Bois Institute for Afro-American Research, is the author of *Thirteen Ways of Looking at a Black Man*; *Colored People: A Memoir*; *Loose Canons: Notes on the Culture Wars*; *The Signifying Monkey: Towards a Theory of Afro-American Literary Criticism*; and *Figures in Black: Words, Signs, and the Racial Self*. He is general editor of the *Norton Anthology of*

African-American Literature and has edited and coedited many other books and special issues of journals. Mr. Gates is a contributing editor for the *New Yorker* and coeditor of *Transition* magazine, which received the 1993 Association of American Publishers Award for "Best New Journal in the Social Sciences and the Humanities." He serves on numerous academic and civic boards and committees, including the Schomburg Commission for the Preservation of Black Culture, the ACLU National Advisory Council, and the Black Community Crusade for Children.

CHARLAYNE HUNTER-GAULT began her career in journalism as a "Talk of the Town" reporter for the *New Yorker* magazine. She worked as an investigative reporter and local evening news anchor for WRC-TV in Washington, D.C., and for ten years as a metropolitan reporter for the *New York Times*, specializing in coverage of the urban black community. She joined "The Mac-Neil/Lehrer Report" in 1978 and was the national correspondent for "The NewsHour with Jim Lehrer" until 1997. Ms. Hunter-Gault is the recipient of numerous awards and honors, including two Emmy Awards and more than two dozen honorary degrees. She is the author of *In My Place*, a personal memoir of her role in the civil rights movement.

HAKI MADHUBUTI, poet, publisher, editor, and educator, has been a pivotal figure in the development of a strong black literary tradition from the sixties to the present. Founder of several independent Black institutions including Third World Press, he has written twenty-one books and is one of the world's bestselling authors of poetry and nonfiction. His *Black Men: Obso-*

lete, Single, Dangerous? (1990) has sold over 750,000 copies. He is an award-winning poet and the recipient of fellowships from the National Endowment for the Arts and the National Endowment for the Humanities. He is professor of English and director of the Gwendolyn Brooks Center at Chicago State University.

Born in 1961 in New Orleans, WYNTON MARSALIS is the most popular and acclaimed jazz musician and composer of his generation and a distinguished classical performer. By force of personality, intelligence, and achievement, he has brought jazz back to center stage in American culture. A longtime recording artist for Columbia Records and Sony Classical, he has performed with jazz groups in thirty countries on six continents. He is artistic director and cofounder of Jazz at Lincoln Center and the recipient of numerous awards and honorary degrees, including eight Grammy Awards and the 1997 Pulitzer Prize for *Blood on the Fields.*

The late Reverend Dr. JAMES M. WASHINGTON, scholar, author, and minister, was professor of religion at Columbia University, professor of church history at Union Theological Seminary, and founder and director of the Robert T. Handy Research Center for the Study of American Church History. He was the author or editor of several books, including *Conversations with God: Two Centuries of Prayers by African-Americans* and *Frustrated Fellowship: The Black Baptist Quest for Social Power,* which was named by *Christian Century* as one of the ten most notable books in the field of religion in 1986.

PATRICIA WILLIAMS is professor of law at Columbia University. Author of the highly acclaimed *Alchemy of Race and Rights* and *The Rooster's Egg*, she is one of the foremost proponents of critical race theory and a powerful voice on the role of race and gender in American law and social justice.

Acknowledgments

THE PATH toward initiating and completing *Restoring Hope* was filled with the hopes, dreams, cares, concerns, worries, and inspiration of so many people around the world that I am moved to write an extended thanks to all. While the book is dedicated to my mother, Dorothy Elaine Batson-Sealey, and the Reverend Dr. James Washington, both of whom left us before it could be completed, in a larger sense, a family of friends and acquaintances helped bring the book to life.

My thanks go first to Cornel West, who while still teaching at Princeton University, in his book-filled office, agreed to work with me on this project. While I was still a virtual stranger, he believed in my vision and helped make it real. His wife, Elleni Amlak, also became a dear friend whom I greatly value. Our editor at Beacon Press, the indomitable Deborah Chasman, bought *Restoring Hope* and let me design it with her support. Tisha Hooks, also at Beacon, provided invaluable advice during the arduous production phases and helped me keep my feet on the ground. Without Marya Van't Hul and Andrew Hrycyna at Beacon, it is hard to imagine how this manuscript would have been produced so beautifully and on time! Gloria Loomis and Carlton Sedgeley gave much of themselves and became key components in the creation of *Restoring Hope*, and I am grateful to them for their help. In her capacity of transcriber, Elizabeth Roach deserves both praise and thanks.

The several dialogue partners with whom Cornel and I worked to produce this volume cannot be thanked enough for their efforts. Dr. Maya Angelou, Harry Belafonte, Wynton Marsalis, Senator Bill Bradley, Patricia Williams, Haki Madhubuti, Dr. James M. Washington, Dr. James A. Forbes, Jr., and Charlayne Hunter-Gault were outstanding participants, sharing with us intimacies of value to both themselves and the world. I am indebted to them all. Sonia Sanchez's poem is yet another one of her miraculous blends of words and emotions for which Cornel and I are deeply grateful.

If the Obsidian Society germinated in my mind and found its first home in the offices of that great independent school known as the Packer Collegiate Institute, it was given birth on the stage of the Schomburg Center for the Study of Black Culture. Dr. Howard Dodson, its chief, and Ms. Roberta Yancy gave me access to their fine institution, and to them I owe a tremendous debt of gratitude. Supporting them ably and with grace were their staff members Curtis Harris and Jerome Jordan. James Briggs-Murry, with his fine audiovisual staff, provided for all our technical needs. Four of the dialogues printed within *Restoring Hope* were public programs at the Schomburg Center, and our audiences were a critical component of the spirit generated in the room as Cornel spoke to our guests.

Were it not for the Packer Collegiate Institute and the faculty and administrators of that 151-year-old institution, the offices of the Obsidian Society and the institutional support I required to function might not have been available. So I thank its headmaster, Dr. Geoffrey Pierson, and staff members Linda Gold, Christine Martin, Roz Seigel, Erland Zygmuntowicz, Donald Odita, Jaki Williams, Anita Halverson, Susan Feibelman, Jenna Laslocky, Richard Eyster, Pauline Orfano, Jeanet Josias, Desiree and Rickford Layne, David Rutherford, and Judith Jones for giving me guidance, critical assistance, and vital support along the way. Former Packer staff who were just as supportive include George Herland, Amy Blumberg, and Lindley Uehling.

My family, both nuclear and extended, also deserve thanks for advice and generosity. My sister, Wendy, and my brother, Gary, must be singled out for praise. My grandparents and the bevy of uncles, aunts, and cousins that make up the GBH clan helped more than they will know to steer me in the direction of success, particularly Allan Batson, in whose homes many of my ideas were conceived, and Ilene Ashby, who helped raise me like a son. I must also mention Paula Greaves and her daughter, Jade, Tracy Hoyte, Dr. June Engle and her husband, Karl Slifer, and their children, Daniel, Joshua, Jackie, and Scott, for being some of the neatest people on earth!

The board members of the Obsidian Society, Inc., and Obsidian, Inc., gave me reason to believe that what I had conceived could actually come into being. In addition to Cornel West, June Engle, and my sister, Wendy, whom I have already thanked, the board includes Sylvia Rhone, Dr. Henry Louis Gates, Jr., Dr. Kassie Freeman, Dr. Gail Foster, Randall Robinson, Richard Parsons, E. Laverne Jones, L. Camille Hackney, Mark Quarterman, David Addams, Leah Johnson, Jeff Scott, Angus Friday, Deirdre Lovell-Othen, and Todd Cranford. Our pro bono counsel at the firm Cleary, Gottlieb, Steen and Hamilton, Yolande Nicholson, Derek Medina, Trecia Canty, and Steve Rabitz, proved themselves unswerving allies, and I remain deeply grateful for their assistance.

A great debt of thanks and praise is owed to my many friends around the world who believed in the long struggle of a fellow traveler and lent invaluable aid. Any list of thanks would be incomplete without saying a few words about Michael Yudell and his wife, Jenny Blasser, Lise-Anne and Scott Putnam, Natalie Monkhouse, Donna Oliva, Sergei Fradkov, Dr. Don Engle, Alan Zawadski and Diane MacCloud, Patrick and Heather Braithwaite and their daughters, Shelby and Riley, Benjamin Exeter, Natalie Minors and her daughter, Julie, Christina Johnson, Jamaal Layne, Zoilo Torres, Sarah Friday, Gillian Friday, Michele Friday, Beverly Renwick, James Shipp, Deirdre Maloney, Shabaki Lambert, Michael and Tammy DeGagne, Lori Minnite, Ann Joshua, Rosemary Kent, Greg and Rita Haines, Suzanne Bruney, Daria Lewis, Raina Lampkins-Fielder, Dr. Chuck Strozier, Dr. Colin Palmer, Dr. Stuart Ewen, Dr. David Nasaw, Dr. Kathleen McCarthy, Juno Diaz, Lizette Alicea, Kim Amprey, Tracy Sherrod, Virginia and Odel Johnson, John Beardman and Laura Collins and their daughters, Cloe and Fiona, Kisha Cameron, Darlene Currie, Jelani DeLeon and her daughter, Kai, Lisa Davis, Janine and Andre Hill and their children, Andrea and Justin, Malcolm Lee, Phil Bertelsen, Stacy Holman, Tinie Evans, Ricky Thomas, Hope Lightbourne, Robin and Jean Renwick and their children, Helen, Vaughn, Lucian, and Randy, Corrine Renwick, Danny Ee, Nick and Deane Andolina and their children, Stephanie and Joe, Joe and Irene Leahy and their children, Loren and Megan, Janet Lowe, Suk Kim, Hakim Quest, Farida Mohammed Ali, Fazeda Mohammed, Shaheba Mohammed, Stradine Prepetit and her children, Christina and Travis, Lisa Pitt, Devlin and Dawn Ponte, Alicia Herelle, Anna Martin, and Josh Hartman.

These people make me happy to be alive, and it is for and with them that I lead my simple life. This is my pantheon of intimates, the first members of the Obsidian Society, and words cannot express my thanks for their presence on earth.

Finally, to my goddaughter, Gabrielle Bruney, just five years old at this writing, and as eager as any child to live a rewarding life, to learn and to grow, I extend my love and commitment to make the world a better place for her, her children, and her children's children.

KELVIN SHAWN SEALEY
8 JUNE 1997

The Obsidian Society

A MAJOR portion of the profits derived from the sale of *Restoring Hope* will be donated to the Obsidian Society and two of its original beneficiaries: the Toussaint Institute Fund (founded by Dr. Gail Foster) and Complexions Dance Company (founded by former Alvin Ailey dancers Dwight Roden and Desmond Richardson).

The Obsidian Society, founded by Kelvin Shawn Sealey in 1995, is a nonprofit grant-making foundation that works in partnership with a group of for-profit sister companies dedicated to its support. Part of its mission—to initiate fundamental shifts in the way consumer capitalism is viewed, while improving the black American condition—represents the modern incarnation of African American self-sufficiency. Its work grows from the impulse that many people of African descent have shared throughout history: to support the collective rather than the individual. At odds with capitalism, the realization of this idea requires courage, altruism, and love, wedded to a promise to stimulate black progress, black hope, and black faith.

Acknowledging the circumstances of capitalist cultural supremacy, the Obsidian Society is building its endowment from profits to be generated in the literary, entertainment, and communications industries. Progressive blackness, indeed progressive *Americanness*, in contemporary pose.

The Society's board of advisors, chaired by Dr. Cornel West, represents a dedicated set of prominent Americans committed to the ideals we espouse. Its mission is to distribute funds in the form of direct cash grants, scholarships, or in-kind gifts to support individuals and institutions whose work contributes to the improvement of black life.

By attempting to raise a considerable portion of its funds through for-profit initiatives, the Obsidian Society hopes to promote this model of capitalism, one which we call "entrepreneurial capitalism." Please send your questions or comments to our web site or address:

The Obsidian Society
170 Joralemon Street
Brooklyn, New York 11201
e-mail: Kelvin_Sealey@Packer.edu
http://www.DreamNet.com or http://www.obsidsociety.org

We invite you to face the challenge with us.

Cornel West, Kelvin Shawn Sealey, and Maya Angelou